GREAT RUGBY HEADLINES

GREAT RUGBY HEADLINES

A Scrapbook of Headlines from the Back Pages

First published in Great Britain in 2002 by
Michael O'Mara Books Limited
9 Lion Yard, Tremadoc Road
London SW4 7NQ

A CIP catalogue record for this book is available from the British Library

ISBN 1-85479-896-0

1 3 5 7 9 10 8 6 4 2

Designed and typeset by Design 23

www.mombooks.com

Printed and bound in Slovenia by Printing House Delo Tiskarna by arrangement with Presernova Druzba D.D.

Extracts, headlines and pictures from the *Daily Mail, The Times, Sunday Times, Sun, News of the World, Guardian, Observer, Sunday Mirror, Mirror, People, Daily Express* and *Sunday Express* are reproduced with the kind permission of, respectively, Atlantic Syndication, News International Syndication, Guardian & Observer Syndication, Mirror Group Newspapers and Express Syndication.

Individual credits: *Observer* © p.28 – report by Robert Morris; pp.38-9, 47 – reports by Clem Thomas; p.39 – photograph by Eamonn McCabe; pp.84-5 – report by Eddie Butler. Allsport © pp.84-5 – photograph by Shaun Botterill; p.93 – photograph by Simon Bruty.

CONTENTS

TWICKENHAM HOSTS INTERNATIONAL RUGBY UNION FIXTURE FOR FIRST TIME

ENGLAND BEAT WALES AT RUGBY: SATURDAY'S CUP-TIE MATCHES.

After an interval of twelve years, England has triumphed over Wales in a Rugby international match. The game was played at Twickenham on Saturday, the score at the call of time being: England, 11 points; Wales, 6 points. (1) A Welsh forward collared. (2) A Welsh player is tackled and falls into touch. (3) Loose play.—(*Daily Mirror* and L.N.A.)

ENGLAND'S GREAT RUGBY VICTORY.

Long Run of Welsh Successes Broken by a Brilliant Win at Twickenham.

FIRST MINUTE REVELATION.

FOOTBALL.
RUGBY UNION RULES.
ENGLAND v. WALES.

England beat Wales on the new Rugby Union ground at Twickenham on Saturday for the first time since 1898 by one goal, one penalty goal, and one try (11 points) to two tries (6 points).

England deserved to win; but there was not much to choose between the two teams, and until the final whistle was blown no one could feel quite sure that Wales might not at least draw level. The weather was unfavourable. A drizzling rain fell throughout the game, and the ground, which was already soft, became in parts a sea of mud, and in these circumstances the game was chiefly confined to the forwards.

English fifteens have often been accused of taking a long time to settle down to their game, but this was not the case on Saturday. Indeed, the beginning of the match was sensational. B. Gronow kicked off for Wales, and the ball went to A. D. Stoop, who ran through to the centre and then punted over the Welsh backs. The Englishmen followed up and tackled their man; there was a scrummage, and then Stoop, getting the ball again, passed to J. G. G. Birkett, who passed again to F. E. Chapman at the right moment and a try was scored. Chapman took the place-kick and only just failed at an awkward angle. After the drop-out England were twice penalized for breaking the off-side rule. There was a deal of keen hard tackling and some good runs by R. W. Poulton and P. Hopkins for their respective sides. England were hard pressed at one point, and from a penalty J. Bancroft nearly kicked a goal. Subsequently England attacked strongly, the forwards playing splendidly and making more than one magnificent rush. Chapman nearly got in again, and soon afterwards he kicked a goal from a penalty awarded for a foul tackle, and England were thus six points up at the end of a quarter of an hour's play. Wales, however, soon reduced this lead. After a fine rush by the forwards R. Owen made a clever feint, and although W. R. Johnson tackled him, in the scramble that followed T. Evans scored a try, which Bancroft failed to convert. Soon afterwards a very fine piece of play by B. Solomon gave England another try, and this was converted. After a rush the ball came through two or three hands to Solomon, who deceived the Welsh backs by feinting to pass, and went over himself. Soon after this the teams changed ends, and at half-time, therefore, England were leading by 11 points to 3.

Wales, however, were by no means finished with. Immediately on restarting they attacked strongly, and within three minutes a beautiful round of passing put R. A. Gibbs, who showed great pace, in on the right, but the kick at goal went wide. Wales still continued to attack, and except for two or three brilliant rushes England were on the defensive most of the second half. The Welsh forwards strove with all their might to overcome the English pack, but although they got the ball frequently the splendid tackling and following up of their opponents and the excellent all-round work done by C. H. Pillman as a winger kept them out; but it was anxious work for England. The Englishmen, however, were attacking when "No side" was called, and amidst a scene of the greatest enthusiasm the teams returned to the pavilion, the jerseys of the Englishmen so plastered in mud that it was difficult to recognize that they had once been white. It was a fine, hard game. The tackling was very keen, but in spite of this there was not a single stoppage for accidents. Mr. J. Dallas, of the Scottish Union, made a strong referee, and several penalty kicks were given against both sides.

England may well be proud of her representatives. It was thought that, with the ground in such a state and with the remembrance of Wales's defeat of the South Africans in the mud at Cardiff Arms Park, the Englishmen would be at a disadvantage; but at half-back and three-quarter back they were better than Wales, and, if the Welsh forwards in the second half held the opposing pack in the tight scrummages and got the ball more frequently, the English forwards were certainly the better in the loose rushes, some of which were really magnificent. Pillman was a great success, and in him England have a wing forward of the type of S. M. J. Woods and F. Evershed. He was taken out of the pack to help in the defence during the last ten minutes, and his pace, dribbling, and tackling were all splendid. It was not a day for outside play, but the English half-backs and three-quarter backs did very well. D. R. Gent was a distinct success, and Owen did not have things at all his own way, with Gent very "nippy" on the ball and with Pillman keeping a watchful eye on him.

Poulton on the left wing had very little to do—it is doubtful if he had the ball more than once during the second half; but Chapman confirmed all the good things that had been said about him. Solomon occasionally held on to the ball too long. His try, however, was a brilliant affair, and on such an afternoon he probably erred on the right side in sticking to the ball. Birkett's inclusion had been much criticized, but his defence was an important factor in England's victory. He has a most powerful "hand-off," reminiscent of G. C. Wade, now Premier of New South Wales, and he was always tackling somebody or breaking up any movement amongst the Welsh backs by his spoiling tactics. Stoop did many good things with the quick instinct of the born footballer, and every one will be congratulating him on the happy result of his captainship.

The hero of the afternoon, however, was undoubtedly Johnson at back. He had a great deal to do, and he did it all splendidly. He fielded the slippery ball accurately; he kicked well, although once or twice he failed to find touch—this was perhaps a failing of the whole of the English back division—and whoever came near him with the ball was certain to fall in a deadly embrace. On Saturday's form he is the best back England has had since Gamlin. The Selection Committee must be well pleased, as they ought to be, with their choice of the fifteen; and after so brilliant a victory over such formidable antagonists they are not likely to make many alterations in the English team for the International matches against Scotland and Ireland.

Wales were very good forward and at back, where Bancroft kicked magnificently; but their three-quarter line was not up to the standard of the Gwyn Nicholls era, nor did Owen and Jones come up to expectations at half-back. Three-quarter backs and half-backs play as a rule as well as their opponents will let them; and it was the fine rushing, following up, and tackling of the Englishmen which made the Welsh backs appear to be below their usual standard.

The stands and general arrangements on the Twickenham ground itself are excellent, but the entrances and exits from the ground are open to considerable improvement. There was quite a nasty crush at the Whitton-road exit at the end of the game, and at least half an hour elapsed before any of the motor-cars or cabs were allowed to proceed on their way home. The approach to the Whitton-road end of the ground is shaped somewhat like the neck of a bottle, and other means will have to be found before the next International match for dealing with the large crowds which nowadays patronize these matches. There must have been 20,000 spectators on Saturday. The sides were :—

ENGLAND.—W. R. Johnston (Bristol), back; R. W. Poulton (Oxford University), J. G. G. Birkett (Harlequins), B. Solomon (Redruth), and F. E. Chapman (Westoe), three-quarter backs; D. R. Gent (Gloucester) and A. D. Stoop (Harlequins), half-backs; W. Johns (Gloucester), H. J. S. Morton (Blackheath), L. E. Barrington Ward (Edinburgh University), C. H. Pillman (Blackheath), E. L. Chambers (Bedford), H. Berry (Gloucester), L. Haigh (Manchester), and D. F. Smith (Richmond), forwards.

WALES.—J. Bancroft (Swansea), back; W. Trew (Swansea), J. P. Jones (Newport), R. A. Gibbs (Cardiff), and P. Hopkins (Swansea), three-quarter backs; R. M. Owen (Swansea) and R. Jones (Swansea), half-backs; J. Webb (Abertillery), I. Morgan (Swansea), C. M. Pritchard (Newport), D. J. Thomas (Swansea), T. Evans (Llanelly), J. Pugsley (Cardiff), H. Jarman (Newport), and B. Gronow (Bridgend), forwards.

Mr. J. J. Dallas (Scottish Union) was the referee.

WALES ACHIEVE FIRST 'FIVE NATIONS' GRAND SLAM TITLE

WALES CHAMPIONS.

Mistaken Tactics by the Irish Forwards— England v. Scotland.

There is no need to enlarge to any extent upon the Cardiff match, which gave Wales the international championship. The game ended pretty much as those of us who had seen the other internationals expected. I thought the Irishmen would have put up a better fight. Still, it is a desperately hard business to win at Cardiff, no international fifteen having been successful since 1899.

Ireland won on that occasion after a great struggle by a try. I think that the Irishmen would have run Wales closer had they not adopted the tactics of pulling Campbell out of the pack, and on that point most writers are in agreement. It is all very well, and often a wise thing to do, to withdraw a man to repel a threatened attack, but it is quite another matter to keep him out practically all through the match.

Ireland weakened themselves at presumably their strongest point, and the addition to the defence did not compensate for the loss forward. In the course of a conversation I had with R. T. Gabe, that famous international observed that the only way to beat Wales is to play them at their own game. England did at Swansea and gave the Welshmen something of a fight. At Cardiff the boot was on the other leg. Wales played Ireland at the latter's own game, and defeated them.

It was something of a novelty to see a Welsh side depending on their forwards to win the game, but that is what happened. Owen and Trew at half had something to say in the matter, particularly the former, but the Welsh three-quarters for them were poor. One would have thought that playing on their own ground the four Cardiff three-quarters would have done better, more especially after the brilliant display they gave at Inverleith.

Ireland made the foolish mistake of relying upon the spoiling, or, practically, the defensive game. Those kind of tactics do not, as a rule, carry a side very far. Perhaps they recalled the fact that they accidentally came off trumps against England, but they would have done better to have remembered how well their three-quarters played against Scotland. Always set out to win, and, if defeat is sustained there is some satisfaction in the knowledge that something definite had been attempted. The loser who is content to ward off his opponent's blows usually gets a good hiding.

R. M. OWEN EQUALS RECORD.

So R. M. Owen, the astute Swansea half, has now equalled W. J. Bancroft's record of having played in thirty-three internationals, and I have no doubt that next season he will surpass it. It is remarkable how so little a man—I suppose he is the smallest half-back taking part in good football—has so long stood the buffeting about that must be endured in an international encounter. He must always be very fit and carry a lot of pluck about with him. That he has escaped serious injury is, I should say, due to his extreme cleverness and adroitness. It is the clumsy man who gets hurt.

Next Saturday at Twickenham the England and Scotland match will see the end of the international tourney, as one may not need to take into account the Ireland-France game on the 25th at Cork. The stakes at issue are the possession of the Calcutta Cup at present held by England, and that mystical trophy known as the " wooden spoon," which Ireland have got rid of.

It is almost idle to speculate upon the probable outcome of the struggle. On the season's form the chances must be in England's favour. England put up a great fight at Swansea, and were a little unlucky to lose at Dublin. On the other hand, Scotland went down badly before the Welshmen and lost on their merits to Ireland. Then there is that defeat in France, which, however, need not be taken seriously.

In this particular game previous form is apt to go by the board. Fourteen years have elapsed since England won at home. That was at Manchester, and there is a legend that the Scotsmen were so sure of winning they omitted to bring the cup with them. It is England's turn to be successful, and I think we shall retain the trophy.

I suppose we shall have the usual pandemonium and excitement at Richmond to-morrow, when Guy's and London fight out the final for the Hospitals' Cup. Guy's, who are the holders, have won it on thirteen occasions and London on five. The display of Guy's against St. Bartholomew's in the semi-final was not convincing, and for my own part I think London will win. Whatever happens, we are certain to see some lively sport.　　　　　　　TOUCH JUDGE.

RUGBY FOOTBALL.
WALES v. IRELAND.

Wales beat Ireland at Cardiff on Saturday afternoon by two placed goals, one penalty goal, and one try (16 points) to nothing, and so regained the International Championship, which they lost to England last year.

THE CROWD.

There must have been close on 50,000 spectators in the Cardiff Arms Park enclosure an hour before the time fixed for starting the game, and it was then decided to close the gates—a wise precaution, since the ground was already overcrowded in every part, and the sweltering masses of people in the cheaper sections were swaying backwards and forwards in a way that suggested the possibility of a serious accident at any moment. The art of laying out a football ground so that the safety and even the comfort of a great crowd may be assured seems to be unknown in Wales; and the Cardiff authorities in particular would find it profitable to inspect some of the amphitheatres in English towns where League teams play to a full house on Saturdays and imitate the arrangments there as far as possible.

In spite of much discomfort, the vast concourse at Cardiff, which included whole regiments of Irish visitors waving green flags and fearing not to talk of '99 (when Ireland beat Wales on that very ground by a try to nothing), was happy and hilarious. When the game was in being the crowd set sound criticism above patriotic ardour; a good piece of work, whether on the part of the men in red or the men in green, was vehemently applauded, and all disinterested persons were delighted with the crowd's impartial enthusiasm and real knowledge of Rugby football. For all that the Irishmen were at first a little bewildered by the ordeal of playing in that pit of eyes and murmurings as of a captive sea. But the soft, holding pitch was a much more serious disadvantage. "In Cardiff when it raineth," as a Welsh spectator epigrammatically observed, and a wet Friday had left the field in a condition which was altogether against the Irish style of forward-play.

THE PLAY.

Wales won the toss and played with the sun behind them, and for a considerable time the Irish backs found it impossible to catch the ball with certainty, with the result that the Welshmen looked likely to score twice or thrice in the first few minutes. Eventually the Irish forwards raised the siege with a characteristic rush, which took the ball right down to the Welsh lines; but the defence was safe, and good touch-kicking soon led to a renewal of the Welsh attack. Campbell was taken out of the Irish pack to strengthen the defence—the fact that Morgan, the Welsh wing forward, was often playing as a kind of quarter-back in combination with the half and three-quarter backs had not escaped notice—and this piece of strategy, although it seemed to kill the passing movements of the Cardiff three-quarter line, caused the Irish forwards to be pushed about in the scrummage and generally beaten for possession of the ball.

The Welsh backs, unable to do much by passing, took to touch-kicking and left the attack to the forwards, who showed excellent form in the loose, often coming away in a close, combined dribble, and once or twice trying short hand-to-hand passing with good results. But for Lloyd's fine kicking Ireland would have been overwhelmed at this stage. Eventually T. Evans charged down Lloyd's kick, and scored a rather soft try, which was converted by Bancroft. Shortly afterwards Hinton hurt his ankle, and left the field for a few minutes; when he returned he was very lame; and this accident had a marked effect on the fortunes of the game, seeing that two of the tries subsequently scored might conceivably have been saved if he had been able to run fast, and the Welsh backs took adroit advantage of the fact that he could only kick with the left foot. Half-time came with Wales leading by five points to nothing, a margin which certainly did not represent their superiority on the run of the play.

Throughout the second half Ireland were manifestly a beaten side; the only question was how much Wales would win by. Even when Campbell was sent back into the scrummage by the Irish captain the Welsh pack was superior at every point of forward play—except at the line-outs—and as time went on their superiority became more and more obvious. The heavy ground and their exertions in the first half had taken the heart out of the Irish forwards, and little or nothing was seen of the fierce rushes for which they are famous. But it cannot be said that the Welsh three-quarter backs made good use of their many opportunities. Owen, who was playing behind winning forwards and having a day out in his 33rd international game, was always giving the ball to Trew, whose admirably varied passes should have meant a small fortune in tries if his three-quarter backs had chosen to make ground by running instead of kicking into touch, or, as happened too frequently, kicking up the field. On one occasion a bout of passing would have resulted in a try if Spiller had gone on instead of sending Gibbs a pass which went high over his head into touch. Shortly afterwards Webb scored after a fine combined rush by the Welsh forwards, but Bancroft's kick at goal was a failure.

Much dull play followed, in which Ireland could make no headway; and there were only Lloyd's touch-kicks and the damaged Hinton's plucky work to arouse enthusiasm until, late in the game, the best piece of passing in the match gave Gibbs the chance of a pretty touch-line run which resulted in a fine try finely converted. A good goal from a penalty kick finished the scoring in a game of little distinction.

A REVIEW OF THE GAME.

The honours of the day, such as they were, belong to the Welsh pack, who worked without a "breather" from start to finish, and were by far the best set of scrummagers seen in this season's international games. The Irish forwards were disappointing in the extreme, but the heavy ground was against them and also the ill-advised depletion of their forces. At half-back Wales had much the best of it; Read, when he was not overwhelmed by the Welsh forwards, was invariably held up by Owen, and it was seldom indeed that the Irish backs, whose defence was sound enough, had a chance of showing that they could give and take passes.

Considering their many fine opportunities, the Welsh backs were a failure; Spiller was the weak point in the three-quarter line, and it is a pity that Birt, a brilliant individualist with a gift for dropping goals at long range, was rejected to make room for him. Bancroft was in his best form, and up to the time he was hurt Hinton was quite his equal. A word of praise must be given to Mr. Potter Irwin (England), who kept the teams in hand and checked certain tendencies in the direction of rough and even ill-tempered play without an inordinate use of the whistle or the infliction of an exasperating number of penalties. The teams were:—

WALES.—J. Bancroft (Swansea), back; J. L. Williams (Cardiff), L. M. Dyke (Cardiff), W. Spiller (Cardiff), and R. A. Gibbs (Cardiff), three-quarter backs; W. Trew (captain) (Swansea) and R. M. Owen (Swansea), half-backs; Ivor Morgan (Swansea), D. J. Thomas (Swansea), Tom Evans (Llanelly), G. Travers (Newport), A. P. Coldrick (Newport), J. Webb (Abertillery), J. Pugsley (Cardiff), and W. G. Evans (Brynmawr), forwards.

IRELAND.—W. P. Hinton (Old Wesley, Dublin), back; C. T. O'Callaghan (Old Merchant Taylors and Carlow), A. R. Foster (Queen's University, Belfast), R. V. Jackson (Wanderers, Dublin), and I. P. Quinn (Dublin University), three-quarter backs; R. A. Lloyd (Dublin University) and H. M. Read (Dublin University), half-backs; G. Hamlet (captain) (Old Wesley, Dublin), M. R. Heffernan (Cork Constitution), T. Halpin (Garryowen, Limerick), C. Adams (Old Wesley, Dublin), T. Smith (Malone, Belfast, and Northern), S. B. Campbell (Derry and Edinburgh University), M. Garry (Bective Rangers, Dublin), and H. Moore (Queen's University, Belfast), forwards.

Referee, Mr. Potter Irwin (England).

ENGLAND WIN FIRST 'FIVE NATIONS' GRAND SLAM HONOURS*

ENGLAND REGAINS THE CALCUTTA CUP.

Scotland Defeated by a Try to 0 at Twickenham, and England Secure the Triple Crown After 21 Years.

England beat Scotland at Twickenham on Saturday by a try (3 points) to nil, and so won the Rugby international championship, as well as regaining the Calcutta Cup. England have won all three matches this year, the first time they have brought off the big performance since 1892. Wales were beaten by 12 points to nil, Ireland by 15 points to 4, and Scotland, as stated, by just one try.

Extraordinarily popular as the win was, the game was a disappointing one. England never played their real game. Individuals might, and did, do brilliant things at times: but, as a side, they were never together. There was a lack of "finish" all through, and Scotland, though they ought to have been well beaten, came within an ace of winning.

Had Bowie, with nobody to beat, gone straight on, instead of cross-kicking he must have scored a try in the second half: scored it, too, probably, in a position from which it would have been easy for Turner to convert.

Scotland were both lucky, and unlucky. Their luck was in the wind. The wind blew almost straight down the ground behind them, in the first twenty-five minutes. Then it went cross-ways: and, in the second half, it changed round again and was almost behind them once more. Their bad luck lay in the crocking of Loudoun-Shand. He was hurt in the last minute of the first half, and for the rest of the match was a mere passenger. Sutherland, who showed great pace in the first half, had to be moved from the wing into the centre, while Shand went outside: and so the really dangerous Scottish wing was absolutely ruined.

The English forwards got the ball cleverly, and heeled quickly, but in the loose they were just lacking in blood. Brown was magnificent, and Ritson did two glorious things: Pillman was fine at times, too. But there was a something lacking, somewhere. In the line-out Scotland ought to have scored heavily, but their forwards, though they kept on getting the ball, knocked on or dropped it forward in the most unaccountable manner.

F. E. Oakeley did splendidly at scrum-half. He was quick and clever and gave his passes at the right height. Davies, however, though great in defence, seemed to have no notion of using his three-quarters. He would either attempt to cut through on his own—and he was so closely marked that that cut never came off—or else he would kick for touch.

Kicking for touch is very nice when you have a long lead, or when using a big wind. But England had not a long lead and the wind was always against them. When Davies did pass it was almost invariably to Poulton: and Poulton's hands, for once, were unsound. He dropped the easiest passes again and again and his extraordinary swerve had been left at home. Indeed, Poulton had a real bad off-day. One was especially sorry for that, because everyone knows that that really good fellow would feel it most horribly himself.

Tarr had not a tremendous lot to do, but what chances he had he took. Tarr, who looks a phlegmatic person, is one of the most unselfish players that ever went on a field. He fed Lowe diligently, passing at the right height and right moment. Lowe, on the right wing, has been badly starved in the other internationals this year. On Saturday he had plenty of chances given him, but J. B. Sweet showed a rare turn of speed, which was rather unexpected, and Lowe was collared again and again when he appeared well off.

Coates, who has been justly called "the find of the year," was in great form again. His trick of apparently offering the left thigh for an easy tackle, and then, with a swing of the body and a heave of the right thigh, shooting a surprised man on to the floor, came off again and again. They marked Coates very closely, so closely that, had Poulton been in form he would probably have scored some three or four tries.

Johnston, as usual, was simply magnificent at full back. For Scotland W. M. Wallace played a brainy game at full back, and his tackling was wonderfully strong and clean. Sutherland gave a lot of trouble in the first half, and was nearly over three times: had Loudoun-Shand not been crocked he might possibly have saved the game for Scotland. Sweet bottled up Lowe well, but, as the Scottish three-quarters consistently stood far too much in a straight line, he was not dangerous in attack. Milroy and Bowie made a good pair of halves, Milroy being particularly good.

The forwards worked all the time but at the finish were done. They had to come back to help the defence, and, of course, that took the steam out of them. They were not as clever as England in getting the ball in the first half, but quite held their own that way in the first twenty-five minutes of the second.

England started to attack, and nearly scored, in the first minute. Then a long bouncing kick, which about four of our backs tried to pick up—and failed to do so—looked dangerous. A foolish cross-kick by Scotland, however, enabled Lowe to touch down. After a quarter of an hour England were in the Scottish "25," and Lowe tried a drop. A minute later Davies, with his three-quarters well set, tried a drop at goal instead of passing: it was such a long way from coming off. A fine run by Lowe nearly ended in a score—Lowe passed in to Davies, who transferred to Pillman: Pillman, however, was well tackled almost on the line. Sutherland looked like getting in a little later, but Johnston seems faster every game he plays, and he just got him in time.

Turner failed from a mark, and Scotland were pressing when Tarr intercepted a pass and with Poulton and Pillman took the ball in to the Scottish "25." Just before half-time Davies passed to Coates, who shoved off two men, and passed back to Poulton: Poulton slung it on to Brown, who fairly took a header over the line and scored. Greenwood failed to kick a very difficult goal.

In the second half, though Shand was practically useless, Scotland dared not take a man out of the scrum. They relied on their forwards to pull them through, and, as it turned out, it was no bad judgment. After twenty-five minutes of even play Bowie had his chance on the right, but he cross-kicked to Sutherland, who failed to gather the ball. From then on England had all the best of it, and Coates, Lowe, Oakeley and then Lowe again made splendid efforts. The tackling, however, was superb. Lowe seemed to score off his last effort, but it was just a touch in goal. Greenwood got the ball from a line out and fell over the line with it: but, as he fell, he dropped the ball. It did look a certain try for a second.

The great crowd was delighted with the English win, but there was not half the enthusiasm one has seen shown in games not a tenth part of this one's importance.

F. B. WILSON.

ENGLAND v. SCOTLAND.
VICTORY OF ENGLAND.

The Calcutta Cup has returned to the possession of England, for Scotland were defeated in a great game at Twickenham on Saturday by one try (three points) to nothing. The Prince of Wales witnessed the game. This was the last of the home international matches, and the winning of it gave to England the full domestic, but not the Imperial, honours of the season—victories over Wales, Ireland, and Scotland, and defeat by South Africa. The annual match against France also fell to England, as usual. The rewards to a team which has been changed very slightly since the opening match include a real cup which they will hold securely until Scotland tries to wrest it from their successors a year hence, and the "Triple Crown," an uncomfortable object, which happily exists only in the imagination of the young. We have to go back to 1892, the year before Wales was discovered by England at Cardiff, for a parallel to these wholesale English victories, and the present occasion is so notable that the matches of the year deserve to be treated by tabular analysis, that fine art of the sister game.

	P.	W.	L.	D.	Points for			Points against		
					G.	T.	P.	G.	T.	P.
England ..	..	3	3	0	0	3*†	6	39	1*	0	4
Wales ..	..	3	2	1	0	4*	2	24	5*†	1	25
Scotland ..	..	3	1	2	0	4	3	29	4*	2	25
Ireland ..	..	3	0	3	0	7*†	0	31	8*†	8	60

*Dropped goal. †Penalty goal.

The only score against England in these matches, it will be seen, was a dropped goal—a mighty kick by R. A. Lloyd for Ireland—for the team, whose attack was as variable as an English summer, have throughout shown indomitable grit with their backs to the wall. Not only were the men outside the scrummage determined tacklers, resolute and fearless in going down to the ball, but the forwards had the admirable habit of breaking up quickly and of dropping back to cover any mistakes of the backs. The eight men, under the immediate leadership of N. A. Wodehouse, stand the strain of comparison with the famous packs led by S. M. J. Woods and J. Daniell; they are not big men, but they held the giants from South Africa in the scrummage, and any disadvantages of bulk and stature found compensation in pace and cleverness; and the season is also notable for the discovery of a great three-quarter back, V. H. M. Coates. Such success as the English teams have had this season could only have been achieved under the best leadership, so let us add to the congratulations showered on Lieutenant Wodehouse, who captained the team throughout the season.

THE PLAY.

Twenty-five thousand people, men and women, packed 16 to the railway carriage, when they had not a motor-car, found their way through a backyard of London to the Twickenham ground. They were revived by Scottish "laments" from a band and a more invigorating March wind which just failed to box the compass. Two minutes of the game banished all thoughts and feelings of discomfort. It began at such pace and with so much wholehearted vigour that the murmur of interest soon swelled to a roar of excitement, which continued with *crescendo* and *diminuendo* to the close. England discovered their game at once—to get the ball out, pass as often as they could, and these tactics were made possible by the excellence of their forwards, who jumped right into their game. They "hooked" the ball three times out of four—their over-keenness to get it was soon checked by penalty kicks for "legs up"—they heeled in so desirable a manner that F. E. Oakeley could hardly have failed to get it away, and away it went merrily with the regularity and precision of clock-work. Sometimes the ball got as far as the outside half-back, more often to a centre-three-quarter back, and very occasionally to a wing man. The English back machinery had broken down, but, in spite of this, the men were always trying, and the play was always open, and provided a wealth of incident which kept up interest and excitement to the close.

The English backs at their best would have put the result beyond question in the first quarter of an hour. Their failure always made it possible that W. M. Sutherland or J. B. Sweet, the Scottish wing three-quarter backs, would, by their dashing play, snatch a victory for their country. It was not until near the end of the match, when the Scottish forwards had shot their bolt and England had settled down to besiege the enemy's lines, that the English backs retrieved their collective character. Then came round after round of passing, which every moment promised success. Each wing three-quarter back got over the line twice, but was flung into touch in goal, an unmarked forward got the ball from a line out, and, though no one was near him, in his excitement lost it as he fell to the ground over the line, and time after time men were tackled or hurled into touch only a few yards out. A brilliant attack was met by desperate defence, and defence won. The whistle came with England only a try to the good, a try scored by L. G. Brown wide out after scrambling play near the line just before the close of the first half, and which J. E. Greenwood failed to convert.

INDIVIDUAL FORM.

R. W. Poulton has done such splendid service for his country this year that his failure in this match was surprising. He seemed quite incapable of taking a pass cleanly, either putting his fingers into the ball or juggling with it until the whistle blew for a "knock-on." Of course, the high wind, which had a shrewd bite in it, made passing difficult; the Scottish three-quarter backs, particularly E. G. Loudoun Shand in the first half, "played on" to him as the known point of danger, while the tactics of W. J. A. Davies, the stand-off half-back, added to his troubles. Behind forwards who played so unselfishly to their backs, the score-sheet would have been vastly different had he played his usual game. Davies had a really bad match, F. E. Oakeley did the "donkey work" with mechanical accuracy, passing at a nice pace well in front of his partner, so that he had plenty of time to get into his stride and plenty of room to move in. Instead of running straight for the line and cutting through or drawing the defence, Davies made a practice of bolting for touch till the men outside him were bunched together and the Scottish three-quarter backs were waiting for them in confidence. If Poulton did not miss the pass the movement often came to a close in or near touch with a loss of ground. Probably Davies will improve with experience: this is his opening year of first class football, and his tendency to selfishness has been acquired, no doubt, by playing for teams in which he had to do all the work. His defence is very sound, and he has the happy knack of falling back at the right time to cover his three-quarters.

Playing under these difficulties F. N. Tarr, V. H. M. Coates, and C. N. Lowe did well. The man of the moment was Coates: he suffered more than Lowe from the short-comings of the men inside him, and was generally so squeezed towards the touch-line that he had to make his own openings. When he got going there was no mistake about his ... although perfectly legitimate, methods, and his play this year should bring back into fashion the old method of handing off which disappeared with A. E. Stoddart and the "three three-quarter" game. Tarr and Lowe played as if they had been partners throughout the season; neither is a showy player, but their methods are effective and show a ripe knowledge of the tactics of the game. Tarr, when the ball came his way in the second half, timed his passes with the nicety which brooked no criticism, and Lowe had his chance at last and proved his capacity. Twice he had hard lines in not scoring.

With R. E. Gordon and W. A. Stewart not available, Scotland were promised a bad time outside the scrummage. Yet they did surprisingly well, especially in defence. E. Milroy could not stop Oakeley from getting the ball away, but he followed its flight and was generally there when tackling had to be done, while his partner, T. C. Bowie, was a sound link in the chain of attack and defence. Had Scotland been served as well at centre three-quarter back as they were on the wings in attack they might have pulled the game out of the fire. Shand did well enough before he was hurt—he was a passenger throughout the second half—but J. Pearson was ineffective. The wing three-quarters, Sutherland and Sweet, were right on the top of their form. Sutherland made one great run from the half-way line which was checked by Johnston at the corner flag, and Sweet, in addition to keeping Lowe in check, did the finest piece of defensive work of the afternoon by running from wing to wing and tackling Coates when he had a clear way to the line. W. M. Wallace, too, at full back, tackled and fielded surely, never losing his head when the pressure was at its greatest.

The Scottish pack, with only two changes, had improved since the game against Wales, but they were again up against better men. The Englishmen, though they were over-weighted, were strong enough to hold their opponents in the scrummage, and were much more clever in getting the ball. In the open the English forwards excelled on the line out and in combined dribbling. The Scotsmen brought off very few of their famous rushes; where they shone was in the loose scrimmages, in which proficiency in the art of "catch-as-catch-can" wrestling is of more importance than knowledge of the finer science of football. Their captain, F. H. Turner, W. D. C. L. Purves, C. M. Usher, and L. Robertson could often be singled out on the lines out, and in the scrambling play which succeeded them. For England L. G. Brown played his greatest game. J. A. S. Ritson and J. A. King also put in some fine work in the open, while every man in the pack except C. H. Pillman, who had an off day, must have done tremendous work to hold their opponents. To her forwards England mainly owes her last and most important victory of the season. The sides were:—

ENGLAND.—W. R. Johnston (Bristol), back; C. N. Lowe (Cambridge University), F. N. Tarr (Leicester), R. W. Poulton (Harlequins), and V. H. M. Coates (Bath), three-quarter backs; F. E. Oakeley (United Services) and W. J. A. Davies (Royal Naval College, Greenwich), half-backs; N. A. Wodehouse (United Services), J. E. Greenwood (Cambridge University), L. G. Brown (Oxford University), C. H. Pillman (Blackheath), J. A. King (Headingley), J. A. S. Ritson (Northern), G. Ward (Leicester), and S. Smart (Gloucester), forwards.

SCOTLAND.—W. M. Wallace (Cambridge University), back; J. B. Sweet (Glasgow High School, F. P.), J. Pearson (Watsonians), E. G. Loudoun Shand (Oxford University), and W. R. Sutherland (Hawick), three-quarter backs; T. C. Bowie (Watsonians) and E. Milroy (Watsonians), half-backs; J. M. B. Scott (Edinburgh Academicals), F. H. Turner (Liverpool), L. Robertson (London Scottish), C. M. Usher (London Scottish), G. H. Maxwell (Edinburgh Academicals), W. D. C. L. Purves (London Scottish), D. M. Bain (Oxford University), and P. C. B. Blair (Cambridge University), forwards.

Mr. T. D. Schofield (Wales) was the referee.

MARCH 15 1913

* England also beat France 20-0 at Twickenham on 25 January 1913; only domestic victories have been noted in the above report.

FIRST INTERNATIONAL PLAYED AT MURRAYFIELD – SCOTLAND WIN FIRST GRAND SLAM TITLE

SCOTLAND REGAINS CALCUTTA CUP

Pulsating Struggle at Opening of New Rugby Ground

LATE DROP GOAL DECIDES

By 14 pts. to 11, Scotland gained a narrow victory over England in the first match played at Murrayfield, the new headquarters of the Scottish Rugby Union.

It was one of the fiercest struggles in the history of matches between these two countries, and the issue hung in the balance until the very last kick.

Ten minutes from the end England led by a single point, but the forwards were by then being outplayed by the Scots, who were scrummaging like tigers. Then, when Waddell dropped a goal a few minutes from the end to give Scotland the lead, there were scenes of frantic enthusiasm.

England opened the scoring through Luddington, who landed a difficult penalty goal after the Scottish forwards had been penalised for offside. The home country went ahead a few minutes

W. E. G. Luddington.

later with the most spectacular score of the match. Macpherson cut through brilliantly and passed to Waddell, who handed on to Nelson, and the scrum-half scored beneath the posts for Drysdale to convert.

Just on the interval clever work by Corbett and Hamilton-Wickes gave the wing three-quarter a chance, which he splendidly seized, to give England a lead of three points, and Luddington added the extra points.

Soon after resuming Corbett again led up to a score. This time he kicked across cleverly and Wakefield got over and touched down after a fine effort. Luddington's kick was charged down under curious circumstances.

The margin was unexpectedly reduced to one point five minutes later, when Wallace sneaked in for a try just by the flag. Gillies took the kick from what looked to be an impossible position, but to the delight of the enthralled Scottish crowd it was successfully taken. From this point to the end it was a terrific struggle, but the younger Scottish forwards seemed to last the pace better.

After one unsuccessful attempt to drop a goal Waddell tried again, and this time succeeded. This turned a deficit of points into a winning margin, and thus gave Scotland the championship and the Calcutta Cup.

Scotland's forwards took a long time to find their feet, but were irresistible in the hard-fought second half.

COTLAND WIN RUGBY FOOTBALL CHAMPIONSHIP

England gain possession of the ball after an exciting moment in a line-out.

One of the English three-quarters is forced into touch.

Smith, Scottish three-quarter, held when trying to gather the ball.

A Scottish defender finding touch with a huge kick. In the background some of the 50,000 spectators.

A splendid view of the great new ground at Murrayfield showing Scotland near the English line just before the decisive goal was scored by Waddell.

ALL BLACKS BEATEN BY ENGLAND, IN ENGLAND, FOR FIRST TIME

ENGLAND MAKE HISTORY

BLACK MARK FOR THE ALL BLACKS
ENGLAND'S TWICKENHAM WIN

English rugby was revealed as formidable by defeat of New Zealand. Team was in great form, and splendid fight by visitors was unavailing. General view (above) shows England player pushed over line near corner flag. Englishmen (right) tackle an All Black.

England well after the ball at Twickenham during their match against All Blacks.

ALL BLACKS BEATEN POINT-LESS FOR FIRST TIME

Prince Obolensky's Phenomenal Speed Gets Two Wonder Tries

By LINE-OUT
England 13 pts., New Zealand 0

THE All-Blacks beaten—for the first time by England in England—and by a Russian Prince. How the vast crowd roared as Obolensky walked quietly back to his position after scoring the second of his two tries. In all my experience of Twickenham crowds I have never heard such a thunderous cheer given to any one individual player.

Other scores came later, but it was Obolensky's two first-half tries that broke the back of the opposition and gave England a six-point lead at the interval.

No one, without possessing the phenomenal speed of the Oxonian, could have scored either of those tries. But Obolensky revealed something more than speed.

In the first instance, he swerved just at the right moment to beat Gilbert; in the second he showed clever football sense in swinging over to the left instead of making for his own corner flag.

This try was actually scored on the opposite wing, and Obolensky thus had swerved and sidestepped his way right across the field.

But Obolensky was not the only hero of England's great victory. The whole team played far above expectation and gave a display that will make Welshmen think again.

ONE TEAM IN IT !

Actually, the forwards did not get so much of the ball in the tight scrums as the All Blacks, but in the loose they held and finally outplayed their opponents.

So far as the backs were concerned there was only one team in it—not the All Blacks. The whole England line ran with rare speed and determination and some of their passing was first-rate.

The tackling, too, was devastating, and not even Oliver could find a way through often enough to threaten any serious danger. He had no Hart outside him to finish off his moves.

Caughey was helpless in the hands of Cranmer, and the wings were well held. Even when Ball did once or twice elude Obolensky, the latter's great speed was sufficient to overhaul him.

Gadney gave a splendid service from the scrum and, though we did not see much of Candler in attack, the stand-off put in some sturdy defensive work.

Cranmer played a magnificent game. He was here, there and everywhere in defence, his kicking saved awkward situations time and again, and one or two of his bursts were tip-top. One of these led to Obolensky's second try. Just after the interval Cranmer took a leaf out of Tindill's book by dummying, steadying himself and dropping a perfect goal.

That made it safe enough for England, but to complete the Tourists' discomfiture, Cranmer brought off another fine break-through and sent Sever racing for the line to score again.

THAT WAS THE END

That was the end, and the All Blacks, for the first time this tour, failed to notch a point. Truth to tell, they never looked like doing so.

Their backs outplayed all through, were forced to run across field most of the time. They looked harmless in attack, and even their attempts at opportunistic efforts were frustrated by the deadly tackling of the Englishmen.

Tindill was not a great success. He tried one drop at goal, but too often ran into the thick of things. Much of the credit for his subjection must go to Hamilton-Hill, who, in his first international, played a sterling game.

Dunkley, Weston, Longland and Clarke also did their share in a great England pack, which had the shove of their opponents.

Owen-Smith played a beautiful game at full-back, never at fault with his fielding and driving back the New Zealanders with long touch-finders.

Altogether a great day for England, and every man deserves his share of the praise which will go to the team for a magnificent victory.

Hats off, too, to the All Blacks. They fought desperately all through and never lost heart from beginning to end.

International Rugger is definitely an outstanding attraction in the world of sport. This view of the crowded car park at Twickenham, for the England v. New Zealand match, tells its own story.

IRELAND BEAT WALES TO ACHIEVE FIRST GRAND SLAM HONOURS

MARCH 13 1948

Rugby International

IRELAND WIN TRIPLE CROWN

Ireland 6 pts, Wales 3

IRELAND'S victory over Wales at Belfast earned for them the triple crown for the first time since 1899, writes W. E. N. Davis.

Wales, however, were perhaps superior in the first half, but there was no doubt about who was on top after the interval. If Strathdee's passing out was erratic the Irish forwards scrummaged better and Ireland had more of the game.

Daly, O'Brien and Mc-Carthy were always prominent for the Irish pack, and Evans (G.), Manfield and Stephens were the pick for Wales.

The game was fifteen minutes old when Ireland took the lead. Kyle sent out a long pass to Mullen, who had to shake off Jones before putting down in the corner.

A try for Wales was well justified when Williams (B.) went over near the post. He beat six defenders to get the points.

Ossie Williams failed with a penalty kick, and five minutes after the change-over O'Hanlon made a strong burst which culminated in Daly crossing over for the deciding try.

FRENCH VICTORY OVER WALES LEADS TO FIRST GRAND SLAM TITLE

THE CAMBERABEROS RIDE ROUGH-SHOD OVER LIONS MEN

WALES SLAMMED

Wales 9 pts, France 14: By TUDOR JAMES

THIS was a fairy tale ending to the story of French Rugby dominance this season.

For the first time in their history the French brought off the Grand Slam with wins against the four home countries.

Wales fell to the fatal combination of the famous brothers Guy and Lilian Camberabero, who made it a memorable farewell match to their international careers.

The only sour note is that the vital French second half try came after at least half-a-dozen of their forwards were offside.

Yet it was the best game of a topsy-turvy season. The fiery French really twisted the tails of the nine British Lions in the Welsh side

FORWARD SUPREMACY

We saw nothing of Welsh centres John Dawes and Billy Raybould in attack, although they defended stoically.

The French had not won at Cardiff for eight years, yet they excelled in the mud.

There was a dramatic turn of events in the second half after Wales had led 9—3.

Said French captain Carrere: "We knew this would be the hardest match of the season. It's always difficult to win at Cardiff."

Not even the skilful hard-working Welsh half backs

Barry John and Gareth Edwards, could produce the spark to fire the team.

It was a mistake not to have brought in Newport centre Keith Jarrett, for the team cried out for a match-winner.

Referee H. Laidlaw (Scotland) made some incredible decisions and failed to see the nudging elbows, late tackles, blind-side punches and, particularly, the French offside tactics.

The French won the line out battles before two forwards were caught offside and Swansea full back Doug Rees put Wales ahead with a 35-yard penalty.

BATTLE OF THE BOOT

Atrocious conditions made it a battle of the boot and the adventurous French soon relised it was as risky as Russian roulette to pass.

In ten minutes Barry John kicked neatly ahead and wing wizard Keri Jones put Wales further ahead with a try

The long loping passes from scrum half Lilian Camberabero to his eager brother Guy had Wales wing forward Dave Moris and John Taylor at full stretch.

In 17 minutes the clever Guy Camberabero dropped a goal to reduce the Welsh lead before the game's greatest winger, Keri Jones just failed in a sizzling race to touch down.

Chink in the Welsh armour is still their line-out work. This handicap is costing Wales dearly.

Full back Doug Rees is growing in stature and started well although he failed later.

There was a mighty roar when he landed his second goal in 37 minutes.

In the 45th minute Guy Camberabero attempted a drop gaol. It was charged down, but Carrere caught the spinning ball to score a try under the posts which Guy converted.

Only a point ahead, Wales now felt a time-bomb was

ticking as the crafty French cleverly made use of the wind

The vital score came in 53 minutes, when Lilian Camberabero scored following an incredible decision by the referee, who failed to see the offside French forwards.

Wales might have surged back, but Rees missed the easiest of penalty goals in front of the posts.

Then the incomparable Lilian Camberabero made it 14—9 with a great penalty goal as France became worthy winners of the five nations championship and the Grand Slam for the first time in 58 years.

WALES.—Pens.: Rees (2); try: Jones.

FRANCE.—Drop goal: Guy Camberabero; pen.: Guy Camberabero; tries: Lilian Camberabero, Carrere; conv: Guy Camberabero.

WALES.—D Rees, K. Jones J. Dawes, W. Raybould, M. Richards, B. John, G. Edwards (capt.), D. Lloyd, J. Young, J. O'Shea, D. Thomas, M. Wiltshire. W. Morris, R. Jones, J. Taylor.
FRANCE.—C. Lacaze, J. Bonal. J. Maso, C. Dourthe, A. Campaes. G Camberabero, L. Camberabero. J. Noble, J. Yachvili, M. Lasserre. A Platnefol, E. Cester, C. Carrere (capt.). W. Spanghero. M. Greffe.

WALES.—Pens.: Rees (2); try: Jones.

FRANCE.—Drop goal: Guy Camberabero; pen.: Guy Camberabero; tries: Lilian Camberabero, Carrere; conv: Guy Camberabero.

WALES.—D Rees, K. Jones J. Dawes, W. Raybould, M. Richards, B. John, G. Edwards (capt.), D. Lloyd, J. Young, J. O'Shea, D. Thomas, M. Wiltshire. W. Morris, R. Jones, J. Taylor.
FRANCE.—C. Lacaze, J. Bonal. J. Maso, C. Dourthe, A. Campaes. G Camberabero, L. Camberabero. J. Noble, J. Yachvili, M. Lasserre. A Platnefol, E. Cester, C. Carrere (capt.). W. Spanghero. M. Greffe.

FINAL TABLE

	P	W	D	L	F	A	Pts
France ..	4	4	0	0	52	30	8
Ireland ..	4	2	1	1	38	37	5
England .	4	1	2	1	37	40	4
Wales ..	4	1	1	2	31	34	3
Scotland .	4	0	0	4	18	35	0

Who wouldn't be worried with the posts so near. And the Frenchman missed his kick, too.

BRITISH LIONS RECORD HISTORIC VICTORY AGAINST ALL BLACKS

Dunedin

HALLELUJAH! Sound the trumpets, bang the drums, crash the cymbals, make any old noise you like! They did it. The Lions did it. They beat the All Blacks in this all important first Test at Dunedin by two penalty goals and a try to a penalty goal, but I hope I never have to live through such a tense match again.

If ever there was a wet rag walking it was your correspondent as he tottered out of the grandstand at the end to pay homage to the magnificent winners; and never before have I kissed a rugby manager, let alone a 17st one like Dr Doug Smith.

It was indeed a famous victory, on good going, won against a mighty All Blacks side that threatened to engulf, and engulf again, but was finally thwarted by the most marvellous covering and tackling I have ever seen.

In front of a record crowd for the ground of 48,000, with 10,000 more locked out and forced to watch the match from the "Scots-

> For the Lions, after losing so many of their top players through injury, it was a day of undiluted glory. They will take some stopping from now on.

men's Grandstands" on a nearby hill and railway line, the All Blacks began as though they were going to demolish the Lions before the latter had even taken breath. For the first quarter of an hour it was as though a colossal pounding machine had gone into action, with the Lions on the receiving end. Wave after wave of All Blacks attacks foundered just short of the line.

But it held magnificently while some of us averted our eyes. Then came the first, and vital, counter-thrust. The Lions won their way to the other end, and an amazing little bull of a man from Scotland had a moment of glory that shall aye endure. John McLauchlan, who prefers to be known as Ian, is only 5ft. 9in. tall and 14½st. in weight—almost a pygmy in the company he was keeping yesterday—and he was packing at loose-head prop against the All Blacks' mastodon, the 6ft. 1in. 18st "Jazz" Muller, who is said to cut the hedge with a lawn-mower. But never once did the "Mighty Mouse" flinch. Indeed, the Lions won the set-scrummage count 24-9, with the help of most of the put-in, and Pullin took the tight-heads 3-1.

This alone would have been a mighty feather in McLauchlan's cap, as it was equally

New Zealand .... **3 pts**
British Isles .... **9 pts**

for Sean Lynch on the tight-head side. But McLauchlan's contribution did not end there. In that 16th minute, when the Lions reached the other end, he got the try that broke the All Blacks' hold at last. It also gave the Lions hope again and altered the whole psychological tenor of the game.

Fergie McCormick, the All Blacks full-back, sent back a pass under pressure to his No. 8 forward, Sutherland, 10 yards from his own line. Sutherland attempted to kick for touch, but there was the "Mouse" up in a flash to throw up his arms, charge down the kick and race after the rebound, behind the line, to score. He looked back from the ground, almost unbelievingly, as the referee awarded the try, and then raced back to half-way festooned with enraptured Lions.

What greater moment could a prop-forward have? Some "Mouse," some man! Tarbolton, Ayrshire, where he was born, and Jordanhill College, his club, where he also learned his physical education, can well be proud. All through he was always the first Lions forward up.

The touring team's battle was not yet over by a long chalk. Barry John missed the conversion of that try, just as he had a couple of penalty shots, and when McCormick equalised with a 25-yard penalty just before half-time, there was nothing in it. McCormick, astoundingly for a man who had kicked a record 24 points for the All Blacks against Wales at Auckland two years ago, had previously missed with a "sitter" from 15 yards and almost in line with the posts.

What is more, he missed another one, almost as easy, in the second half, and altogether had a disastrous day—not that anyone minded after last week's Lions match against Canterbury.

Apart from his missed goal-kicks, McCormick was tantalised all through by some wonderful clearing touch-kicking by John. The fly-half, who saved the Lions time and again, making distances of up to 40 yards, almost always seemed to make the ball land just across the touchline, only a foot or two from McCormick's grasp. John indeed was once again the controlling genius behind the Lions scrum, though this time defensively, not in attack.

In the face of wave after wave of thunderous crashing and bashings by the All Blacks forwards he kept his cool and sent them packing with one raking touch-finder after another, until they finally had to give him best. On top of this it was he who

got the two penalty goals which sealed the All Blacks' doom. One was from 35 yards, in the 14th minute of the second half, the other from 40 yards three minutes from the end; and they were both beautifully struck from considerable angles. Until that second penalty, the second half had seemed the longest I have ever known.

The All Blacks forwards were still pounding away. For 20 minutes they kept the Lions penned in their own quarter. The New Zealanders were winning the line-outs handsomely. At the end the count in their favour was 26-12, thanks largely to Kirkpatrick's palming back at the end of the line. They also won the rucks 15-7, but here the Lions fought back to the end, with McBride a giant in this as in other phases of play.

But the most wonderful part of the Lions performance in that endless second half was the heroic tackling by Gibson and Dawes in the centre and the covering work by the three

> I hope I never have to live through such a tense match again. If ever there was a wet rag walking, it was your correspondent as he tottered out at the end.

loose forwards, Dixon, Mervyn Davies and Taylor. Then there was John Williams at full-back, playing the game of his life, catching towering up-and-unders, taking fearsome punishment from the All Black forwards and always coming up for more.

"It was spirit that did it," said Dawes afterwards, and so, for all to see, it was. The All Black backs had endless ball, but they had neither the skill nor the pace to round the tigerish Lions defence in midfield.

Whenever a try threatened there were two or three Lions there to seal off the gap, and always John and his kicking.

I have not mentioned Gerald Davies and Bevan on the wings; "Chico" Hopkins, who substituted for Gareth Edwards at scrum-half after 10 minutes; or Delme Thomas in the pack. But believe me, they all earned their full share of the collective glory, and none more so than Hopkins.

It was known in advance that Edward was a risk, with a hamstring injury received in training. So it was no surprise to those in the know when he had to come off Hopkins stepped into the breach superbly and kept nagging away at Syd Going righ to the end.

GRRREAT
Wonder Lions thrash All Blacks

Sound the trumpets—
They did it!

A Union Jack is waved, the All Blacks are beaten and John Dawes calls for a handclap for the vanquished

"We were beaten by a better side." They took their chances where we didn't," said Colin Meads afterwards. A gracious admission—and let no one say that Meads is finished. He was immense again yesterday.

For the Lions, after losing so many of their top players through injury, it was a day of undiluted glory. Now they are in the series right to the end—even if they lose the next two Tests and no one here will admit that they can.

As Dr Smith said, with a sidelong smile, at the after-match reception: "You can say I am reasonably satisfied." Then, to the Lions: "Training at nine-thirty in the morning!" The spirit in this side was something to wonder at even before the game started. Now it has soared to the firmament.

They will take some stopping from now on.

New Zealand: W. F. McCormick; R. A. Hunter, B. G. Williams, W. D. Cottrell, K. R. Carrington; R. E. Burgess, S. M. Going; No. 8, A. R. Sutherland; Second Row, I. A. Kirkpatrick, C. E. Meads (capt.), P. J. Whiting, I. A. M. McNaughton; Front Row, B. L. Muller, R. W. Norton, R. A. Guy.

British Isles: J. P. R. Williams; T. G. R. Davies, C. M. H. Gibson, S. J. Dawes (capt.), J. C. Bevan; B. John, G. O. Edwards; T. M. Davies; Second Row, P. J. Dixon, W. D. Thomas, W. J. McBride, J. Taylor; Front Row, J. F. Lynch, J. V. Pullin, J. McLauchlan.

Referee: J. G. Pring (Auckland).

JOHN SPARKS AMAZING WIN

New Zealand 3 pts, British Lions 9

IT'S victory — an incredible glorious, triumph for Lions in their first Test in New Zealand.

In the dressing-room where manager Dr. Doug Smith had issued an "England Expects" message, there were scenes of great jubilation after one of the greatest wins in British Rugby history.

In twenty test matches in New Zealand the Lions had won only two. To win the first of a series is unique.

It was a David and Goliath story, for the All Blacks had almost a stone a man advantage in weight.

CLEAN GAME

Forecasts of a blood bath were off beam. Except for a few flurries of fisticuffs it was a remarkably clean game

Luck was on the Lions side for the All Blacks had most of the game.

Interest here in the match was fantastic. There was a crowd of 46,000. At least 10,000 failed to get in while the surrounding hills were crowded with people.

The feat seemed impossible in the first torrid minutes as the fearsome All Blacks showed their tremendous power.

In wave after wave of attacks the thin red British line held out.

After ten minutes fate dealt the Lions a cruel blow. Key man Gareth Edwards went off with hamstring trouble. To reserve Ray Hopkins' eternal credit it was Twickenham of two years ago all over again—as he raced on as substitute to play a hero's role in the glorious victory

The All Blacks' threatened massacre fizzled out as Lions flexed their muscles to fight back

It had seemed certain that the incredible power of muscle man Colin Meads and his heavyweight forwards would crush the Lions

The New Zealanders were winning line-outs with painful regularity, while the ball came out of the rucks on the enemy side like a golden egg being laid.

With such possession the British mission seemed hopeless.

British resistance never buckled or broke. Centres Mike Gibson and John Dawes and the gallant back row of Peter Dixon Mervyn Davies and John Taylor were always running in for possession and tackling tigerishly.

UNCANNY TOUCH

King Barry John wore the crown as proudly as any monarch. His inch-accurate touch - finding, his uncanny anticipation of danger, took the heart out of the New Zealand pack.

John became executioner of New Zealand's hopes of scoring tries.

As the victory champagne was flowing Frank Kilby a former All Blacks captain, told me that John is the greatest player he has seen in forty years and the Lions side can win a Test series for the first time.

Almost overcome with joy, skipper John Dawes said it was amazing how the Lions withstood extreme pressure to come back and win.

Even the controversial All Blacks' coach, Ivan Vodanovich, praised the British side and added: "Rugby was the winner today. We missed two fairly easy chances and you cannot afford to miss goals or tries in Test matches."

Culprit of the missed kicks was full back Fergie McCormick, who notched a world record 26 points against Wales in New Zealand two years ago

LAST MATCH

It's probably McCormick's last game for New Zealand because, in comparison to skilful, courageous and dynamic John Williams, he was a failure.

It was an amazing performance by the trail blazing sons of Britain after losing their Test props, Ray McLoughlin and Sandy Carmichael, in the ill-fated Canterbury game.

A close kept secret was that Gareth Edwards injured his leg in a training session and Hopkins had been tipped off to stand by.

Edwards told me: "It's the old hamstring trouble and it would have been fatal to try to carry on. I will be right in a few days."

So the slam-bang boys of Britain thunder on in the knowledge that even injuries cannot halt their match-winning crusade.

The All Blacks were so eager to restore their image, shattered in South Africa.

They attacked in swift deadly bursts with the remarkable 35 - year - old Meads always leading.

In their wings Bruce Hunter, an 800 metres champion, and Ken Carrington, they had match winners, but they were denied the ball.

Clever scrum half Syd Going, pumped out the passes for the flood which seemed certain to engulf Lions.

Very much against the run of play Britain were ahead in sixteen minutes when the "mighty mouse," Ian McLaughlan, scored a try. He was the game's best forward.

Then the All Blacks big guns opened up and Britain were under siege

McCormick lost the game for New Zealand Arrogantly he tried to drop a goal instead of placing a penalty and then missed another two sitters.

For once luck was favouring Britain.

Lions wing Gerald Davies showed flashes of genius and almost scored a try, while John Bevan was surprisingly subdued.

WINNING KICKS

McCormick equalised with a penalty goal before man of the match Barry John clinched victory with two penalty goals.

Everyone was bubbling over with zest after an historic match.

Coach Carwyn James said : "It's the culmination of a full year's preparation." Manager Smith said the game was a shot in the arm for Rugby

In eleven games the Lions have scored a fantastic 291 points. It was their first win at Carisbrook for forty years.

So the relentless Lions roar on. Maybe to make history by winning a Test series in New Zealand.

It's one in the bag and three to go

Determination And British Lion McLaughlan means to get his hand on the ball.

Lions too good for us, admits Meads

New Zealand 3 British Lions 9: from PAT MARSHALL

DUNEDIN, Saturday. Hallelujah, we did it! Yes, what New Zealand coach Ivan "the Terrible" Vodanovich predicted would be a Passchendaele turned out to be a Waterloo. The thin red line held, and as the Duke of Wellington said, "'Twas a damned close run thing."

Lions skipper John Dawes did not phrase it quite that way, but he did say with utter relish: "I am absolutely delighted we won. It was a great game played as Rugby should be played, but, most important, Rugby was the victor."

A modest fellow, Dawes. He did not think to mention his thin red line of heroes who met the greatest battering I have seen any international side take without so much as bending. And that hard, ruthless but great sportsman Colin "Pinetree" Meads agreed.

This victory by a try and two penalties to a penalty was *deserved*. "You must know it's damned hard for me to say this," Meads told me, "but we were beaten by a better side."

Maybe the real clue is that the All Blacks didn't win the tight scrums.

For this we can thank two stand-in props, Ian McLaughlan and Sean Lynch, and the quiet Englishman, John Pullin. Pullin won the tight head count three to two, but the biggest victory was that of McLauchlan.

MASSACRED

At 14st. 6lb., he took on and massacred 17st. 10lb. Brian "Jazz" Muller in the greatest David v. Goliath contest I have seen on a Rugby field. What is more McLauchlan scored the only try of the match.

It came in the 16th minute. After an initial battering, during which time Gareth Edwards pulled out with a damaged hamstring muscle to be replaced at scrum-half by Chico Hopkins, the Lions went into their first serious attack.

John Williams came into the line to feed left wing John Bevan. Bevan got in an inside punt to the line, which full-back Fergie McCormick fielded in goal, McLauchlan was on him like a flash, but McCormick got in a hurried pass to Alan Sutherland.

McLauchlan was far from finished. He harried Sutherland, charged down his kick, and dived on the ball for a try. Barry John missed the conversion, but it made no difference.

"King" John utterly demoralised poor McCormick with some of the most devastating line kicking I have seen in 25 years of Rugby reporting. Though he levelled the score before half-time with a penalty given against Dawes for lying on the ball, McCormick also missed two absolute sitters.

Not so John. He slammed over two second-half penalties from 35 and 45 yards to seal the victory.

NEW ZEALAND.—W F McCormick: B A Hunter, B G Williams, K C Carrington, W D Cottrell, R Burgess, S M Going, A R Sutherland, I A Kirkpatrick, C E Meads (captain), P J Whiting, A McNaughton, B L Muller, R T Norton, R Guy.

LIONS.—J P R Williams; T G R Davies, C M H Gibson, S J Dawes (captain), J C Bevan, B John, G Edwards (R Hopkins), T M Davies, J Taylor, W J McBride, W D Thomas, P J Dixon, I McLauchlan, J V Pullin, J F Lynch.

Gibson is grabbed and there's more New Zealand help close at hand.

LIONS BECOME FIRST BRITISH SIDE TO WIN TWO TESTS IN NEW ZEALAND

John fires Lions All-Greats

New Zealand 3pts, British Lions 13

RING out the bells. Let joy be unconfined. British Rugby took a giant leap forward with this history-making victory by becoming the first Lions in the annals of world Rugby to win two Tests on New Zealand soil.

Now New Zealand can only hope to draw the series in the final game at Auckland on Saturday week.

Every Britisher here was celebrating, from Alun Talfan Davies, the Recorder of Cardiff, to the newest immigrant in this Rugby stronghold

With fifty other Welshmen Mr Davies had made the twelve thousand mile journey and saw his son-in-law, Barry John, play the greatest game of his life.

In three matches on this famous ground the fabulous John has scored an amazing fifty points to push his tally for the tour to a remarkable 167 points.

Fifteen British heroes have gained immortality. This marriage of brilliant and individual skills and team work can spell doom for the All Blacks in the final game, which can produce a first-ever Lions victory in a Test series.

FABULOUS FORWARDS

British hearts were pounding with pride for eight magnificent forwards who more than held their own against the awesome All Blacks

We have heard about the "terrible eights" of the past.

There has never been a better pack of British forwards.

Said delighted skipper John Dawes: "We knew if we could share in possession our brilliant backs would win."

Coach Carwyn James praised the British new boys

and said Gordon Brown had provided power in the second row with Willie John McBride while Derek Quinnell had kept the All Blacks match winner Sid Going under constant pressure and had broken the vital link in the New Zealand chain

Etched indelibly on everyone's memory is the performance of Gareth Edwards, who played his best Test match, scoring and making a try.

Due to Gareth's speed and guile the Lions were thirteen points up in eighteen minutes.

Said Welsh selector Cliff Jones: "It is a privilege of a lifetime to be here. British Rugby has at last come good because of coaching techniques and Carwyn James."

LUCKY CALL

Lions coach James revealed that winning the toss was all important.

The plan was to play with the notorious Wellington wind behind them.

He telephoned the met office and learned the wind would die in the second half.

Said James: "We wanted quick scores and played to run and run with the ball in the second half. It worked like a dream."

New Zealand skipper Colin Meads told me: "It is the best ever side to visit New Zealand — and that includes the 1956 Springboks."

When the roll was called at the hotel before the match Barry John and John Bevan were missing.

They were stuck in the lift between floors and had to climb out.

The game opened explosively. An amazing fifty yard run by Gerald Davies in three minutes fizzed up into a movement in which Barry John dropped a thirty yards goal.

It was Davies in full flame of genius. A savage side step cleared him of a covey of defenders.

He was at it again as he scored the try which Barry John converted after the ball had hit the post and bounced the right way.

Davies must be the best

wing in the world, for his defence is so secure.

Amazingly, the All Blacks were being beaten at their own game as Britain began winning the rucks.

Heart, head and hub of the British side was Gareth Edwards who displayed all his qualities of skill and speed.

He sent Barry John over for the try which John converted and the Lions had their lucky thirteen points in the bag.

Superbly led by Willie John McBride the forwards were fighting fire with fire and scorching the favourites.

Laurie Mains scored a try early in the second half and then it was feared that ten points lead for the Lions might not be big enough.

But the British defensive screen with John Williams always the monarch became impregnable and with John Dawes and Mike Gibson tackling tigerishly the thin red line held.

Gibson put in one remarkable seventy yard dribble which would have done George Best proud.

EQUAL MERITS

Despite it all Colin Meads set a fine example, well supported by the controversial Brian Lochore the All Blacks late substitute.

But McBride and new boy Gordon Brown equalled the New Zealand he-man for size and efficiency. And won the scrums.

A moment of anxiety came when Barry John and Gerald Davies collided and were partially stunned as the All Blacks lost their clever flyhalf, Bob Burgess, who went to hospital with concussion.

Referee John Pring, who might get the final test did a good job in several explosive moments.

Once he gave New Zealand a penalty and then reversed the decision when McLaughlin was kicked.

In twenty New Zealand games the Lions have scored a fabulous 471 points.

British giants go roaring into history

Mike Gibson about to gather the ball and set another Lions' attack in motion against New Zealand.

Willie McBride gets in a nifty pass back following a line-out and Gareth Edwards is away despite attention from All-Black Guy.

❝ WE MADE HISTORY TODAY. WE'RE NOW THE FIRST LIONS TEAM TO AT LEAST DRAW A SERIES IN NEW ZEALAND ❞

—CARWYN JAMES

BRITISH LIONS BEAT SPRINGBOKS FOR FIRST TIME ON SOUTH AFRICAN SOIL

PHIL BENNETT
. . . three penalties

South Africa 3 British Lions 12

THIS BRILLIANT victory by the British Lions on the muddy bog of Newlands will reverberate from Cape Town to High Veld with the resonance of thunder. For this was the first time ever that a Lions pack have trampled Springbok forwards into their own Kikuyu turf.

Granted the margin was only three penalties and a dropped goal to a dropped goal.

But the scoreline does not reflect the complete, utter superiority of mighty Willie-John McBride's men.

"We played it exactly as we wanted to and controlled the game from start to finish," chortled happy Lions coach Syd Millar as his mud-spattered heroes trotted off while the weary Boks trudged behind shoulders - hunched, heads down, after losing their first Test to the Lions since 1955.

Millar, who schemed the game

From Sunday Express Reporter, Cape Town, Saturday.

with McBride and Gareth Edwards, had summed up perfectly.

Apart from the opening 25 minutes, with a strong wind at their backs, the Springboks were hardly ever in the hunt. With Edwards and Phil Bennett, relentlessly kicking in support their pounding pack drove them backwards, backwards, ever backwards.

The Springboks had only one hope against this thunderous driving urgency—they had to run the ball. But such was the stranglehold of the Lions pack and, so complete their control, that the Boks scarcely got any ball to run.

When they did they were cut down like ripe corn by devastating tackling.

The heroes? It's difficult to nominate individuals but Ian "Mighty Mouse" McLauchlan in the front row, McBride and Mervyn Davies were outstanding up front and Roger Uttley looked perfectly at home on the flank.

Behind, Edwards stole the show and conducted the orchestra with aplomb, flair and brilliance.

Bennett, too, rose to the big occasion , placing his penalty goals with almost professional detachment as if he had never looked up the word "failure" in his dictionary.

J. P. R. Williams was also his usual ice-cool self. But they were all heroes and they played superbly as a team.

They made just one mistake in the game and this led to the Springboks' score.

In the 18th minute Springbok full back Ian McCallum was wide with a 50-yard penalty. J. P. R. Williams, instead of touching down, decided to run the ball but left J. J. Williams stranded in goal and he was forced to kick to touch in goal.

From the five-yard scrum the Boks won quick ball and their fly-half Dawie Snyman dropped a 30-yard goal.

OFFSIDE

That was their last taste of honey. In the 34th minute their centres were caught offside in front of the posts and Bennett booted his first penalty for the Lions to turn level 3—3 with the wind now in their favour.

Five minutes after half-time Bennett booted them into the lead when Springbok skipper Hannes Marais was offside at a ruck 30 yards out. Then 20 minutes later Bennett goaled penalty No. 3 after one of the Boks was offside at a scrum. Gareth Edwards applied the coup de grace to the stricken Springboks with a great 35-yard drop goal 10 minutes from the end.

● Mike Gibson, of Ireland, is to join the Lions party, it was announced yesterday. Gibson, who will be a replacement for injured England fly-half Alan Old, will be with them on Friday, June 21, a day before the second Test in Pretoria.

Lions smash the bogey

Magnificent Lion Gareth Edwards (third from left) roars through the Springboks to launch another attack

GARETH TURNS ON MAGIC FOR SUPER LIONS

Eight cheers for this unbeatable Lions pack

S. AFRICA 3 pts., BRITISH ISLES 12

EIGHT rousing cheers for the Lions! That's one for every member of Willie-John McBride's magnificent pack.

They produced one of the greatest forward displays ever seen at muddy Newlands. The Springbok forwards were smashed aside like schoolboys.

Willie-John's wizards were backed to the hilt by Phil Bennett, who kicked three penalties.

And by scrum-half Gareth Edwards who banged over a superb dropped goal from 30 yards when time was running out.

FEARSOME

That made it 12-3 to the Lions . . . and the Springboks didn't have an earthly.

No wonder the South Africans are now trembling at the fearsome might of the Lions' pack who clinched Britain's first Test win in this country since 1955.

No wonder coach Syd Millar was over the moon. "We played the game as we wanted and controlled it from start to finish," he said.

FROM ROY CLARKE Cape Town, Saturday

The Lions, with a strong wind at their backs in the second half, has such control that the Springboks were only able to invade their territory three times

The Lions were guilty of one lapse which gave the Springboks the lead after 23 minutes.

Full back Ian McCallum missed with a a 50-yard penalty, but instead of safely touching down, John Williams tried a cross scissor movement with J. J. Williams.

Williams, with the Springboks bearing down on him, was forced to kick hurriedly and the wind took the ball behind.

From the five-yard scrum the Springboks won the ball and Dawie Snyman dropped an excellent goal.

Phil Bennett missed his first penalty kick at goal but it nearly led to a try as Mervyn Davies charged down the clearance kick and was stopped only a yard short of the line.

The Lions' control of the tight scrums was superb

● *PHIL BENNETT . . . kicks killed the Boks.*

and Gareth Edwards had plenty of time to decide what tactics to use.

It was 3—3 at half-time and from the moment Bennett drove the Springboks back to their own line with a long penalty early in the second half, it was obvious the Lions were on their way to a historic victory.

South Africa rarely managed to gain possession and when they did use their backs, they found the Lions defence too formidable.

BRITISH ISLES: J. P. B. Williams; W. Steele, I. McGeehan, R. Milliken, J. J. Williams; P. Bennett, G. Edwards; I. Mc-Laughlan, R. Windsor, F. Cotton, W. J. McGride (captain), G. Brown, R. Uttley, M. Davies, F. Slattery.
SOUTH AFRICA: I. McCallum; G. Muller, P. Whipp, J. Oosthuizen, C. Pope; D. Snyman, R. McCallum, T. Saurman, P. Van Wyk, H. Marais (captain), J. Williams, K. De Klerk, J. Cotzee, M. Du Plessis, J. Ellis.

Gareth masterminds triumph in the mud

by Vivian Jenkins

South Africa 3pts
British Isles 12pts

ROLL the drums, bang the cymbals—the Lions are on the warpath again. They beat the Springboks in the first international of the four-match series at Cape Town by three penalty goals and a dropped goal to a dropped goal.

So they are off to a flying start in their bid to become the first touring team since the turn of the century to beat the Springboks in a series in their own country.

There was no doubt about the quality and justice of the win. On a mud-bespattered pitch after torrential overnight rain, they made every use of the best weapons at their disposal. These were the might of their heavy pack, led by the evergreen Willie John McBride on his record-breaking 71st international appearance (57 for Ireland and 14 for the Lions) and the superlative brilliance of Gareth Edwards at scrum half.

The Lions produced a tightly-controlled and superbly efficient

> This was not the rugby of the dazzling free-running 1971 Lions in New Zealand, but in such conditions the touring side had no option but to play as they did

display. This was not the rugby of the dazzling free-running 1971 Lions in New Zealand, but in such conditions the touring side had no option but to play as they did.

"We played it exactly as we intended to," their widely-smiling coach, Syd Millar, said afterwards, "and controlled the play all through." That was perhaps being a little over-exuberant because the Springboks in the first half fully held their own and were in no way flattered by the half time score of 3-3.

Dawie Snyman, their fly half, had dropped a splendid goal after 23 minutes and Phil Bennett replied with an easy 20-yard penalty goal six minutes before the interval.

At that stage the game was still wide open, but the Springboks had had a strong wind in their favour, which advantage went to the Lions in the second half.

From that point they continued with the same tactics—all-out forward play with controlled rucking and the ever-present Edwards behind them, booting the ball upfield. Some of his kicks were high "steeplers," others superbly clever rolling efforts with top-

spin, which eventually bobbed into touch and gained ground untold for his side.

It was Edwards, too, who dealt the final blow to the Springboks. In the 28th minute of the second half from a ruck 35 yards out following a line-out, he turned on his heel and let go a magnificent drop-kick between the posts.

Until then the Springboks were still in with a chance at 9-3, following two further penalty goals by Bennett. Both were splendid efforts, from wide angles near the 25 and with the muddy ball.

Bennett played an admirable game all through, fitting into the general pattern as laid down by the coach and making many astute tactical kicks himself, especially in the closing stages.

But it was Edwards, at scrum half, who was the real hero of the day. Apart from his dropped goal, which clamped the lid down on the Springboks, he was tireless in defence and saved many an ugly situation when the Springbok forwards, more particularly in the first half, were on the rampage.

John P. R. Williams, at full-back, was another telling agent in the Lions' win. Ice-cool, and completely unflappable, he caught all the high kicks that came his way and returned them with interest. And Williams showed admirable restraint in cutting out his normal adventurous running, so conforming with the general pattern of the Lions' tactical scheme.

It goes without saying that every member of the Lions pack earned his full share of glory for this immensely encouraging start to the real business of the tour.

This was no insignificant Springbok pack, averaging two pounds per man more than the Lions forwards. The first half was a real "ding-dong" with each side struggling for the mastery.

All the more credit, then, to McBride and his men that they gradually began to get the upper hand. In the last 20 minutes, with a stamina that betokened extreme fitness, they were carrying all before them.

McBride himself, Gordon Brown and Mervyn Davies were in unstoppable form and won the decisive line-outs 28-20. Hooker Bobby Windsor signalled his British Isles debut by sharing

the tight-heads 2-2. For this, obviously, full credit is due to his props, Fran Cotton and Ian McLauchlan. Fergus Slattery and Roger Uttley on the flanks completed as fine a battling pack as the Lions have ever produced.

Uttley played a stormer and the experiment of using him as a flanker was justified up to the hilt.

The three-quarter line, inevitably in a game such as this, hardly figured in attack, but in defence they were up on their opponents like rockets. Milliken and McGeechan in the centre, must have bruises galore on their shoulders after all the crunching tackles they brought off.

For the Springboks the outstanding players were the two brothers, Ian and Roy McCallum, at full back and scrum half respectively.

Ian McCallum was as cool as his opposite number, John Williams, and under much more pressure, especially in the closing stages, while Roy was the authentic

> Edwards . . . was the real hero of the day. Apart from his dropped goal, which clamped the lid down on the Springboks, he was tireless in defence and saved many an ugly situation

indiarubber-man, bouncing up indefatigably under all kinds of pressure.

The Springboks tried their best to run the ball at times, but the Lions defences were too well organised for them.

This is the first time the Springboks have lost to the Lions at Newlands since 1938 and it is the first time, too, that the Lions have won the first international of a series against them since the unforgettable 23-22 match at Johannesburg in 1955.

The omens, in other words, are set upliftingly high and the Lions go into the rest of the series in immense heart.

SOUTH AFRICA—1. McCallum (Natal); C. Pope (Western Province), J. Oosthuizen (W. Province), P. Whipp (W. Province), G. Muller (Transvaal); D. Snyman (W. Province), R. McCallum (W Province); No 8, M. du Plessis (W Province); Second Row, J. Ellis (SW Africa), K. de Klerk (Transvaal), J. Williams (Northern Transvaal), J. Coetzee (W. Transvaal). Front Row, H. Marais (Eastern Province, capt), J. Van Wyk (N Transvaal), J. Sauerman (Transvaal).

Dropped goal: Snyman.

BRITISH ISLES—J. P. R. Williams; W. C. C. Steele, I. R. McGeechan, R. A. Milliken, J. J. Williams; P. Bennett, G. O. Edwards; No 8, T. M. Davies; Second Row, R. M. Uttley, G. L. Brown, W. J. McBride (capt), J. F. Slattery; Front Row, F. E. Cotton, R. W. Windsor, J. McLauchlan.

Dropped goal: Edwards. Penalty goals: Bennett 3.

Referee: M. Baise (Western Province).

LIONS RECORD SECOND VICTORY OVER SPRINGBOKS IN SOUTH AFRICA

LIONS CRUSH BOKS !

Mauling for Springboks

South Africa..... 9 pts	British Lions..... 28

ROBERT MORRIS

PRETORIA, 22 June
TWO UP with two to play—that is the happy position in which the Lions find themselves tonight after their win by a goal, four tries, a dropped goal and a penalty goal to two penalty goals and a dropped goal—the biggest defeat the Springboks have ever suffered at international level.

On a sunlit field here this afternoon, the Springboks had improved their set scrummaging by the changes they had made from the side who played in the first Test two weeks ago, and they also won a lot of possession from the line-outs, but the Lions used their pace to spoil the Springboks' halves, and then when the Lions got the ball, they brought their pace, their wit and their teamwork to bear on the game with some prolonged running and passing which the 'Boks just could not match.

The Lions relied on the punting of Edwards and Bennett, but they were quick to seize any clear opportunities for running and passing.

In the end, the Springboks were forced to try to run with the ball, but though some of their three-quarters looked strong runners, their handling was technically poor and they showed little judgment of when to pass. Eventually they were disorganised by injuries which forced them to bring on two substitutes—McCallum, who had been badly shaken earlier, went off midway through the second half and was replaced by Dawie Snyman, the man who played at stand-off half in the first Test. He was only on the field for a few minutes before he had to be carried off on a stretcher with a leg injury.

The Springboks now moved Whipp to full-back and brought on Leon Vogel. The Springboks were well beaten, however, before McCallum went off—the Lions were already leading 18—9 and were looking thoroughly cool and in control.

The Lions also had their injuries—Phil Bennett hurt an ankle in scoring a try, and Edwards briefly took over the job of goalkeeper. Milliken also played for a while at stand-off half, but Bennett was running and kicking again before the end.

It was a strange game with no obvious pattern, and with the Springboks winning plenty of the ball but doing very little with it, the Lions seldom won clean possession from the line-outs. But their solidity at the set scrums provided the platform from which Edwards and Bennett could do their devlishly accurate punting. When the ball was loose, the Lions proved the quicker thinkers and the better judges of the most effective move to fit the moment. Their first try, after thirteen minutes, came when Edwards kicked the ball up the left touch-line from a scrum and the ball bounced kindly for J J Williams who scored.

Then the whole Lions side seemed to handle in one all-enveloping, sweeping counter-attack, involving notably McBride twice, Edwards, Davies and Uttley, and J. J. Williams ran over for another try, this time on the right. Bennett converted this try with a fine kick, and though Bosch then dropped a goal from a line-out for the Springboks, the Lions were well placed with a lead of 10—3 at half-time.

Two minutes after the interval, a penalty goal by Bosch made it 10—6, but then the Lions pulled away with eight points in five minutes from two tries. First Slattery ran round the blind side of a maul and sent Phil Bennett scampering off on a run in which he dodged past several defenders and finally turned inside the last Springbok for a grand try. Then Bennett tackled Bosch and, under pressure, another defender kicked wildly so that Edwards was able to race for the line before transferring to Brown, who hurtled over.

Another penalty goal by Bosch made it 18—9, but then McGeechan dropped a goal from a line-out, Bennett kicked a penalty goal and the Springboks were thoroughly demoralised. In injury time, Milliken got over for yet another try for the Lions. So the Lions scored five tries to the Springboks none. You couldn't ask for anything more conclusive than that.

Lions—J P R Williams, J J Williams, I R Mcgeechan, R A Milliken, W C C Steele P Bennett, G O Edwards, I Mc Lauchlan, R W Windsor, F E Cotton, W J McBride (capt), G L Brown, R M Uttley, T M Davies, J F Slattery.

South Africa—I McCallum, G Germishuys, P Whipp, J Snyman, C Pope, G Bosch, P Bayvel, H Marais (capt), D Frederickson, N Bezuidenhout, K de Klerk, J Williams, J Ellis, D McDonald, M du Plessis.

Lions rip up the records

WILLIE JOHN McBRIDE
... successful Lions skipper.

PRETORIA, Saturday
CALL them the greatest British Lions of them all ... the fifteen heroes who destroyed South African Rugby pride here today.

Call them the record-breakers ... the wizards who inflicted on the arrogant Springboks their heaviest - ever defeat at home.

They became the first touring side to go two-up in a series in South Africa this century and took their tour aggregate to 425 points .. a British record with ten matches still to play.

It was a five-try wonder show and the tears of remorse were flowing here tonight in this hot-bed of Afrikaan nationalism.

Powerhouse

But it was champagne all the way for the roaring Lions, now poised to win a Test series in South Africa for the first time this century.

And those who accused them after the first Test of being negative and intent only on victory were made to eat their words

They called them the "reserves" when they came out here, but these British backs have proved dazzling match-winners on

S. Africa 9pts, British Isles 28

South Afica's hard grounds. Even brilliant Irishman Mike Gibson will be pushed to claim a place in the remaining Tests.

Phil Bennett had already missed a penalty chance when Gareth Edwards, his Welsh scrum-half partner, opened the floodgates with a typical piece of magic.

He chipped cleverly over the scrum near the South Africa line and Llanelli wing John J. Williams fell on the ball as it rolled over the line. First blood to the Lions, and much more to be spilled.

The Springboks gave a 60,000 crowd brief hope of success with 10 minutes of constant pressure, generated by a determined pack, but it was like trying to stop an avalanche with a thimble.

After 29 minutes, Bennett burst clear inside his own 25 on a jinking run and John J. Williams again crossed after the ball had passed through numerous

pairs of hands. Bennett converted.

The Springboks retaliated with a drop goal by fly-half Gerald Bosch seven minutes before half time for the teams to turn at 10—3.

Two minutes into the second half, there seemed just a chance that South Africa could hang on when Bosch bagged a penalty but seven minutes later came the beginning of the end.

Chance

A 50-yard scoring movement began when Englishman Roger Uttley wrested possession up front. Fergus Slattery kept the movement going to Bennett who ignored winger Billy Steele to jink inside for a try.

It was a fabulous effort from the little Welshman, so heavily under fire before the first Test only a couple of weeks ago.

The game cascaded away from the South Africans like a runaway waterfall and Edwards took advantage of a poor clearance to put Gordon Brown over South Africa's only

JOHN L. WILLIAMS ...
scored two tries

answer to this superlative Rugby seemed to be the boot of Bosch, and he kicked a 60-yard goal with 17 minutes left, to make it 18—9.

Scot Ian McGeechan made it 21—9 with a dropped goal and with just over two minutes left Bennett popped over a penalty after a late tackle by Springbok Leon Vogel.

To the shattered Springboks, once world champs now Rugby's tattered tramps, it must have seemed the final straw.

But in the fifth minute of added time, Dick Milliken, the Irishman who has improved so much on this tour, jinked in for the fifth try.

Scorers.—South Africa: Penalties Bosch (2): dropped goal. Bosch. British Lions: Tries, J. J. Williams (2), Bennett, Brown, Milliken: con., Bennett: penalty, Bennett: dropped goal, McGeechan.

TEAMS

SOUTH AFRICA.—I. McCallum; G. Germishuys, P. Whipp, J. Snyman, C. Pope; G. Bosch, P. Bayvel; J. Marais (capt.), D. Frederickson, N. Bezuidenhout, K. de Klerk, J. Willims, J. Ellis, D. McDonald, M. du Plessis.

BRITISH ISLES.—J. P. R. Williams; J. J. Williams, I. R. McGeechan, R. A. Milliken, W. C. C. Steele; P. Bennett, G. O. Edwards; J. McLauchlan, R. W. Windsor, F. E. Cotton, W. J. McBride (capt.), G. L. Brown, R. M. Uttley, T. M. Davies, J. F. Slattery.

J. J. WILLIAMS
—two-try hero.

GARETH EDWARDS
—strong, surging runs.

Terrific, Lions—you are just unbeatable

BRITISH LIONS WIN 1974 TOUR SERIES AGAINST SOUTH AFRICA

Two-try Williams clinches series

PORT ELIZABETH, Saturday.—The British Lions are Rugby champions of the world! They smashed the once invincible Springboks into ignominious and humiliating surrender here in the bubbling cauldron of Boet Erasmus Stadium with a devastating display of power Rugby to record their 18th successive victory.

Now, an untouchable 3—0 up in the series, they are ready to whitewash the sad, dejected South Africans in the Fourth and last Test at Johannesburg on Saturday week.

And I can see nothing to stop them maintaining their unprecedented unbeaten record and becoming the first touring side to win a Test series in South Africa this century.

ELATION

As the 200-odd ecstatic British supporters and the coloured section went wild with elation the Lions team picked up captain "Willie" John McBride to chair him off in their moment of triumph.

"The greatest moment of my life," said the beaming McBride. "Now I can die happy. We did what we came out to do. Nobody knows the loyalty I got from every player. Mission completed."

Springbok depression, after losing the first two Tests, sank as deep as a goldmine with this latest massacre. Ten changes—they have used 31 players in the three Tests—snowed the panic of the Springbok selectors.

But for the first half they

South Africa 9   British Lions 26

from JOHN REED

looked a rejuvenated side showing fire and aggression at forward that pinned down the Lions.

However such was the control, discipline and drill of this Lions pack, the dedication of the whole team, the mobility and teamwork, that they took a firm, iron grip just before half time. And in the second half they ground the Boks into the dust with a performance that even surpassed the brilliance of John Dawes' 1971 historic triumph in New Zealand.

Two ugly punch-ups, one in each half illustrated the determination of McBride's heroes. The Lions were clearly going to stand no nonsense and it was the rough South African lock "Mona" van Heerden who had to be carried off with injured ribs in the second half.

This was certainly the best Lions scrum I have ever seen. And as Irish coach Syd Millar — who, with his Ballymena club "twin," McBride, and Welsh

tour manager Alun Thomas, had planned it all—said afterwards: "The forward control was magnificent."

"The backs also took their chances superbly and overall our second half display was the best of the tour."

It is almost invidious to single out individuals. But the flying Welsh left wing John J. Williams scored two more tries to add to the brace he got in the Second Test—the first time a Lion has scored four tries in a series against South Africa.

MAGNIFICENT

Scotland's Andy Irvine, introduced to the right wing as kicking cover to fly-half Phil Bennett also played his part nobly by kicking two penalty goals, one from 57 yards, and converting one try.

And Bennett, himself, got two dropped goals, while that magnificent lock Gordon Brown got a try.

All the Springboks could offer in return were three penalty goals by fly-half Jackie Snyman —and tonight the nation is in mourning while the Lions celebrate with champagne.

SOUTH AFRICA : Tony Roux ; Gert Muller, Peter Cronje, Jan Schlebusch, Chris Pope ; Jackie Snyman, Gerrie Sonnekus ; Nick Bezuidenhout, Piston Van Wyk, Hannes Marais (captain), Polla Fourie, Moaner van Heerden, Johan de Bruyn, Jan Ellis, Johan Kritzinger.

LIONS : John Williams ; Andy Irvine, Ian McGeechan, Dick Milliken, John J Williams ; Phil Bennett, Gareth Edwards ; Fran Cotton, Bobby Windsor, Ian McLaughlin, Willie John McBride, Gordon Brown, Roger Uttley, Fergus Slattery, Mervyn Davies.

Referee : Cas de Bruyn.

SUPERB LIONS CLINCH SERIES

South Africa 9
British Lions 26

THE LIONS plucked the most precious jewel from South Africa's Rugby crown in Port Elizabeth yesterday.

They became the first international side to beat the Springboks in a series this century, having roared to their third successive Test triumph before a wildly partisan crowd.

And whatever happens in the final match of the series, Britain have decisively usurped the title of world champions from the fanatical 'Boks after a tense and often brutal encounter.

Yesterday's three tries to nil drubbing of South Africa made it a giant tour triumph for those two mighty Britishmen with a huge appetite for success, skipper Willie - John McBride and coach Syd Millar.

Now all that remains is the tour whitewash . . . and with four matches left — including one Test — who can doubt that they will do it.

South Africa had said they would not surrender

MY BALL, MY SERIES—Lions skipper Willie John McBride (headband) moves in to take the ball from Van Heerden.

without a fight . . . and they were true to their word. But some of the incidents yesterday may leave a sour taste even in their mouths.

The first came five minutes before half-time when Springbok Tonie Roux kicked ahead, Johan Kritsinger gathered and was sent crashing a yard from the Lions' line.

Punches

In the resultant pile of bodies, players from both sides began trading punches before referee Cas de Bruyn stepped in to sort out the trouble.

Eight minutes into the second half the match again boiled over after a clash between Gordon Brown and Polla Fourie. As the players exchanged blows, Fergus Slattery joined in the fighting and several players again became involved before the referee intervened.

The Lions were not to be intimidated. They had fought tooth and claw for success and even the hard men couldn't ease their grip on this match.

Again the mighty men up front made it all possible, containing a fierce Springbok opening and providing enough possession for Gareth Edwards and Phil Bennett to parade their skills after the interval.

The names of the Lions

heroes slip easily off the tongue. Phil Bennett, carrying a still injured foot but able to land two killer second-half dropped goals.

Scot Andy Irvine, who took over the goal-kicking from Bennett and landed two penalties and a conversion. And wizard wing John Williams, who scored two sizzling tries to add to his two second Test touchdowns.

South Africa promised an early assault, and backed by the presence of Prime Minister John Vorster, delivered it.

They were ahead after six minutes when fly-half Jackie Snyman popped over a penalty. But the Lions came storming back to level after a quarter of an hour

when Irvine hammered over a kick from eight yards inside the South African half.

The Springboks were exerting all the pressure and missed two vital kicking opportunities. Three minutes before half time, the Lions snatched a shock lead to signal the beginning of the end for the hard men of South Africa.

Brown picked up a loose ball from a line out in injury time and ran five yards for the simplest of scores. Irvine missed the conversion, but the Lions led 7—3 at half-time.

Easy

Irvine made amends five minutes into the second half with a prodigious penalty from two yards inside his own half.

Bennett dropped a goal to make it 13—3 and create the platform for Williams' two tries. For the first he appeared from nowhere to take from full-back John Williams and dash over.

For the second he ran 45 yards, beating several defenders, before kicking over full back Roux, picking up and touching down. An Irvine conversion and Bennett dropped goal completed the Lions scoring, while Snyman landed two more goals for South Africa.

SCORERS.—South Africa: Pens, Snyman (3). British Lions: Tries, J. J. Williams (2), Brown. Pens, Irvine (2). Con, Irvine. Dropped goals, Bennett (2).

LIONS ARE RUGBY KINGS

CHAM PRID

WILLIE-JOHN McBRIDE . . . as Lions' captain he is three Tests up with one to go.

South Africa 9, British

THE AMAZING British Lions can prou champions after inflicting another hu once-mighty Springboks.

The Lions now lead 3—0 in the four Tes South Africans h lost a series at ho since 1896.

THE TEAMS

SOUTH AFRICA: A. Roux; G. Muller, P. Cronje, J. Schlebusch, C. Pope; J. Snyman, G. Sonnekus; N. Bezuidenhout, P. Van Wyk, J. Marais (capt.), J. van Heerden, J. de Bruin. J. Ellis, P. Fourie, J. Kritzinger.

BRITISH ISLES: J. P. R. Williams, A. Irvine, R. Milliken, I. McGeechan, I. J. Williams; P. Bennett, G. Edwards; J. McLaughlan, R. Windsor, F. Cotton, W. J. McBride (capt.), G. Brown, R. Uttley, F. Slattery, M. Davies.

Referee: C. de Bruyn.

And if anyone dou that the British are top of the world, lis to former All-Black Scott, who saw the Li win in New Zealand 1971.

He said: "These are greatest Lions ever."

In 18 unbeaten mat they have shown claws and roared

'NOW I CAN DIE HAPPY' SAYS WILLIE

PION — OUR
E OF LIONS

themselves world
ng defeat on the

first time that the

☆

es — but never have
y played with greater
racter than in this Test.

t the end, these magnifi-
t men were doing as
y liked, running the
ingboks dizzy with their
erbly controlled play.

t was team work and
fidence that enabled the
ns to withstand severe
t-half pressure.

The Springboks, after
king 11 changes, showed
at physical determin-
on, if little else, in a
to win.

This physical approach
to two ugly incidents,
e in each half, when
re was a general free-for-
among the forwards.

RETALIATION

n the past, Lions for-
rds would have walked
ay, for the sake of good
ations.

Not this mighty pack.
ey raced to the aid of a
icken colleague and gave
re than they got in
urn.

The Springboks were
aken to find themselves
iling 7-3 at half-time,
ter giving so much effort.
But the Lions took it all,

BLEDDYN WILLIAMS REPORTS

Port Elizabeth, Saturday

and gradually the forwards
—and "the general" scrum-
half Gareth Edwards—took
command.

The Springboks had
opened the scoring with a
fourth-minute penalty by
Snyman, but Irvine, who
played splendidly on the
wing, equalised with a
penalty 12 minutes later.

ROCKED

The Springboks were
rocked in the third minute
of first-half injury time
when Gordon Brown scored
a dramatic try straight
from a line-out.

And they were positively
floored by Irvine's second
penalty, a monster 58-yard
effort five minutes into the
second half.

It was a killer—and the
Springboks reacted, as expected, with a show of
violence.

But the Lions just kept
getting better. Bennett
dropped a goal to make it
13—3 and then came one
of the truly great tries.

From a line-out on the
Springboks' ten yard line,

Edwards sent the ball spinning along the line.

McGeechan missed out
Milliken to find J. P. R.
Williams in support.

The fullback put J. J.
Williams clear and then
took a return pass. He gave
it back to the Llanelli
winger who scored between
the posts for Irvine to convert.

J. J. soon followed that
with a second great try.
He ran 45 yards before
kicking ahead and gather-
ing to score in the corner
to make it 23—9.

Snyman had kicked two
late penalties but the
Springboks were now a
shattered side.

And Bennett, although
still not fully fit, capped a
fine game by kicking a
second dropped goal.

Skipper Willie-John Mc-
Bride said later: "Now I
can die happy. We did
what we came to do."

Manager Alun Thomas
called it "the best per-
formance of the tour," and
coach Syd Millar said:
"The forwards were even
better than in the Second
Test."

*"DOC" John Williams
. . . one of the Test stars*

McBride's pric

Brave Lions roa

e and joy—

PRIDE, misery, and joy. Lions' captain Willie John McBride (left) salutes the efforts of the British Lions after their record-smashing Third Test victory in South Africa yesterday. "Now I can die happy," said McBride. And live joyfully too. . . "We'll go on a bender," he promised. Joy in the face of Lion Gordon Brown (right) who scored the first try and knows he has a place in history. Misery? That's man-in-the-middle Springbok centre Peter Cronje squeezing in to a gap that never existed on the field. Said McBride: "I asked the boys not to let our advantage slip. I reminded them that the job wasn't finished." The Lion-Hearts answered his call.

REPORT—PAGE 38

nto history

WALES DOMINATE BRITISH RUGBY, WINNING 4TH CONSECUTIVE TRIPLE CROWN

FINEST HOUR

CROWN WALES AGAIN

Wales 27 England 3

TWO TRIES in just over a minute from forwards Mike Roberts and Paul Ringer swung Wales towards another Triple Crown triumph at Cardiff Arms Park.

Those tries came as Billy Beaumont's England side were battering away in the second half at a Welsh lead of 7—3.

And when J. J. Williams crossed for a third try soon after, the whole of Wales was singing.

J. P. R. Williams, leading Wales for the last time, had limped out of the game just before that three-try burst.

The tension was there from the opening minutes when Alan Martin and Nigel Horton, the big opposition lock forwards, swopped blows. England flanker Tony Neary was equally active with his fists a moment later.

BLEDDYN WILLIAMS REPORTS

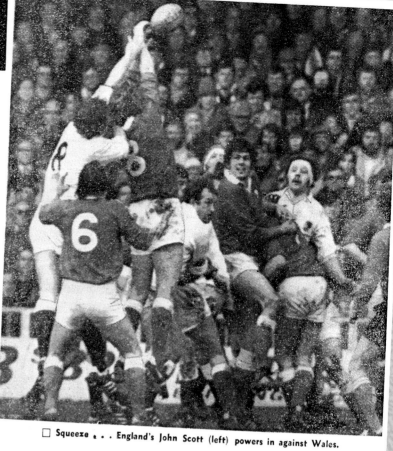

☐ Squeeze . . . England's John Scott (left) powers in against Wales.

It's a five-try super show

The sides soon settled down and Neil Bennett, the England fly half, missed a long-range penalty.

In a snap counter-attack Gareth Davies got Elgan Rees away but the flying Neath wing put a foot in touch when he might have given Wales the lead.

SHORT

Fenwick was also short with a long-range penalty, but Cardus knocked on and from the scrum under the England posts Gareth Davies dropped a fine goal.

A dash from a line-out by Mike Rafter and a wild back pass by Welsh skipper J. P. R. Williams put his side in trouble. Then when Fenwick fell offside at a line-out, Bennett failed miserably with a 26-yard penalty.

Fenwick was equally guilty with a penalty miss for Wales, but this was from 45 yards. All the football was coming from Wales, prompted by Holmes and Davies at half-back, and England were kept busy in defence.

Beaumont and his England forwards were finding the greatest difficulty in getting into the game as Welsh pack leader Derek Quinnell urged on his men. As a result the England backs were constantly battling to keep their line intact.

Fenwick missed another kickable penalty before England were able to relieve the pressure but even then it was only momentarily for the Welsh forwards soon stormed back.

They won two magnificent rucks in succession and from the second Holmes put his backs away with J. P. R. Williams moving smoothly to the line.

PENALTY

J. P. R. swivelled and put Richards through for a great try.

A minute later Wales were penalised for blocking, and Bennett, with his fourth attempt, landed a 30-yard penalty to put England back into the game.

Gareth Davies, who took over the kicking from Fenwick, then missed a penalty.

A magnificent break by Holmes from a scrum 40 yards out should have led to the second Welsh try, but Richards put a scoring pass to ground.

Wales continued the pressure and Fenwick missed yet another penalty, so the 7-3 half-time score in no way showed how much they had commanded the match.

Six minutes into the second half England were penalised for collapsing a scrum, but this was not Fenwick's day.

He needed just three points to break the home international points scoring record but was again well off the mark with a kick from 52 yards.

Then, as the strong sun broke through, England at last began to put their game together.

Bennett missed a drop goal attempt and then another penalty. But England kept up the pressure and so nearly scored when Cardus broke away from a ruck. It took some strong defensive work by J. P. R. Williams to save Wales.

INJURED

He was hurt in that tackle and left the field for good with Llanelli's Clive Griffith coming on for his first cap.

COMMAND

Wales were now in full flight, with their forwards in absolute command, and shortly afterwards J. J. Williams seized on a Richard pass for a great try.

Martin converted with a magnificent kick from the touchline and Wales rejoiced.

Wales crowned a magnificent all-round performance with a fifth try by Rees, that Fenwick converted.

Victory gave Wales their fourth consecutive Triple Crown and fourth Championship in five years.

Williams's departure was the signal for an all-out onslaught by the England forwards, but they failed to break a very resolute defence.

Then back came Wales to make the game safe. A charge by Squire and a magnificent diagonal kick by Gareth Davies put them in a commanding position.

From a line-out that followed, Roberts made a fairy tale return to international Rugby by forcing his way over for a try. Like the first, it went unconverted.

Then J. J. Williams picked up a loose ball on the left, throwing an overhead pass to Fenwick. He ran cleverly before sending Ringer over.

WALES

J. P. R. Williams 8
Rees 7
Richards 8
Fenwick 7
J. J. Williams 7
Holmes 7
*DAVIES 9
Richardson 8
Phillips 8
Price 8
Martin 8
Roberts 7
Ringer 8
Squire 8
Quinnell 8

ENGLAND

Hignell 7
Squires 7
Cardus 7
Dodge 7
Slemen 7
Bennett 7
Kingston 7
Smart 7
Wheeler 7
Pearce 7
Beaumont 8
*HORTON 8
Neary 7
Rafter 7
Scott 7
Referee: J. P. Bonnet (France) 7

Wales scorcher

FINAL TABLE

	P	W	D	L	Pts
Wales	4	3	0	1	6
France	4	2	1	1	5
Ireland	4	1	2	1	4
England	4	1	1	2	3
Scotland	4	0	2	2	2

New jewels in a f

Exit J.P.R. the Valiant

CLEM THOMAS in Cardiff

Wales . . . . 27 pts   England 3

ENGLAND'S hopes of sharing the championship fell prostrate as Wales, with overwhelming talent, retained the diadem in scoring two goals, three tries and a drop goal to a solitary penalty goal. Wales thus won the championship with their most convincing performance of the season, and the Triple Crown for an unprecedented fourth consecutive year.

It was never really a contest apart from a 10-minute period in the second half when England gave some acount of themselves. Their forwards did not reach the heights of their performance against France. A well-organised, disciplined Welsh pack had problems only with their throwing-in at the line-out. Quinnell marshalled his forwards beautifully. They responded with their best-controlled ball-winning of the season.

Mention must be made of a marvellous return to the international scene by Mike Roberts, who responded to his critics by winning some essential early line-outs, lasting the pace like a youngster and capping it all with a try. Another impressive Welsh forward was Ringer, who produced a fantastic work-rate. But the hub of the Welsh triumph, which provided their biggest victory over England since 1905, when the winning points margin was 25 points, was the strong, composed play of their young half-backs, Holmes and Davies.

The strength and ability of the former, who was made the Man of the Match by the journalists, and the elegance and grace of the latter, look like gracing the scene for another decade. Fenwick, whose kicking prowess deserted him, managed to equal the record number of points in a home international season, and he had a hand in three tries. His co-centre, Richards, brought a sharp cutting edge to the Welsh midfield which had been long absent.

J. P. R. Williams, in his last match for Wales, was injured at the beginning of the second half, and left the field to have eight stiches put in hight calf. But before his departure his great qualities were in no way dimmed by time and he remains the most valiant player I have seen in a Welsh jersey. No player deserved more to go out on the highest of notes as captain of a Triple Crown and championship side.

Of England, it is sad to record that the magic of the National Stadium was too inhibiting to allow them to raise their game in the manner they achieved against France, chamiponship runners-up. Perhaps they were unfortunate that Horton, in the middle of their pack, did not seem fully recovered from his hamstring injury. Only their back row at times showed moments of quality; Scott, in patricular, had a good match.

The English halves never ssettled into any fluency. Their centres looked leaden-footed. Subsequently, the strength of their wings, Squires and

INTERNATIONAL TABLE

	P	W	D	L	F	A	Pts
Wales	4	3	0	1	83	51	6
France	4	2	1	1	50	46	5
Ireland	4	1	1	2	53	51	4
England	4	1	1	2	24	52	3
Scotland	4	0	2	2	48	58	2

Slemen, was never put to the test.

There is no greater occasion for Welsh supporters than England playing at the National Stadium, especially when it is for the Triple Crown and the championship. And when the English scent the possibility of usurping Welsh rule, you have the ingredients of a nerve-jangling experience.

The sun peered tentatively through the tundra-like conditions of the last few days, and the firm ground was made for kicking as Wales kicked off. The first line-out brought a niggling outburst between Horton and Martin. Early indications were that Wales were in control and it was they who were stretching the ball to the wings.

After 12 minutes a towering penalty kick by Fenwick was knocked on by Cardus and, from the resultant scrum, Wales calmly organised a drop goal which Gareth Davies put over with ease and nonchalance. England had a chance to level the score when Fenwick was offside from a line-out. Bennett missed the 25-yard penalty. Fenwick did likewise from 30 yards.

Welsh confidence began to show when J.P.R. Williams ran the ball out from his own '25'; Wales were firmly back in the England half. Another fruitless exchange of penalties by Bennett and Fenwick followed.

The crunch came for England after 32 minutes when Quinnell charged through the middle and rolled to create a ruck. The ball was put into the England '25' when Squire won the ball, J. P. R. Williams coming into the Welsh line and rowing a tackle to feed Richards, who broke a brittle-looking defence and burst over for a try.

Bennett kept England in touch with a 30-yard penalty after Roberts, who was having a tame time in the line-out, was offside in a ruck. Holmes made the cleanest of breaks when, wtth the greatest of certainties, Richards put down the pass. Wales might have led by more than 10 points at half-time. That would have been a more accurate measure of their superiority.

Wales again began dominceringly in the second half, but after Fenwick missed his fifth penalty England at last tried to impose some authority on the game. They could provide no finish, and Bennett missed again with a drop goal and a penalty. It was England's turn to throw away a glorious opportunity when Cardus broke keenly but elected to kick for the corner when there were men outside him.

JPR Williams was injured and went off. England made a series of individual onslaughts on the Welsh line. Perhaps it was a turning-point when Ringer and Fenwick nailed Hignell, raising the siege, and Clive Griffiths, of Llanelli, came on for his first cap to replace JPR.

Gareth Davies found a beautiful touch on the England corner flag, where Horton palmed down for England, but Roberts crashed through and poached a try. Soon after, J. J.

urth Welsh crown

† AMONN McCABE

Johnny the Jumper : Scott, of England, way over the heads of the Welsh pack at Cardiff.

Williams slipped Squires and, when checked by Hignell, threw an overhead pass to Fenwick, who drew his man and put inside to Ringer, who capped a marvellous afternoon's work by scoring a try.

The Welsh were off the rein, and again it was Fenwick who switched the attack for Richards to show his dazzling pace to put J. J. Williams over in the corner. Martin, with his first kick of the game, converted handsomely from the touchline.

England were in rags. Substitute Griffiths showed his quality when he picked up a difficult ball on the half-volley to surge through the England defence and kick ahead for Rees to get the touch-down, and for Fenwick to make his only successful kick of the game, which

brought him level with Tony Ward, Roger Hosen and Phil Bennett as the only players to score 38 points in an international season.

Wales — J P R Williams (Bridgend, captain) ; H E Rees (Neath), D Richards (Swansea), S P Fenwick (Bridgend), J J Williams (Llanelli) ; W G Davies (Cardiff), T D Holmes (Cardiff) ; J Richardson (Aberavon), A Phillips (Cardiff), G Price (Pontypool), M G Roberts (London Welsh), A J Martin (Aberavon), J Squire (Pontypool), D L Quinnell (Llanelli), P Ringer (Llanelli).

England — A J Hignell (Bristol) ; P J Squires (Harrogate), R M Cardus (Roundhay), P W Dodge (Leicester), M A C Slemen (Liverpool) ; W N Bennett (London Welsh), P J Kingston (Gloucester) ; C E Smart (Newport), P J Wheeler (Leicester), G S Pearce (Northampton), N E Horton (Toulouse), W B Beaumont (Fylde, captain), A Neary (Broughton Park), J P Scott (Cardiff), M Rafter (Bristol).

Referee — J-P Bonnet (France)

ENGLAND LACK VITAL TOUCH OF CLASS

1980 FIVE NATIONS: ENGLAND OUTCLASS IRELAND AT TWICKENHAM

At last! England come good

By ROY CLARKE England 24 Ireland 9

ENGLAND'S long-promised rugby revival finally arrived at Twickenham yesterday.

Not since Richard Sharp's side last won the championship 17 years ago has an England pack of forwards been so completely in command.

Bill Beaumont's eight produced so much power in the scrums that Ireland were humilated and left in tatters.

The green shirts were shunted yards on England's put-in at the scrums and wheeled on their own.

Three great England tries—all immaculately converted by Hare—were scant reward for a side so relentlessly in charge.

Beaumont, the great Fran Cotton and new cap Phil Blakeway were all magnificent in the tight phases and the recalled Nigel Horton imperiously ruled the lineouts.

But, as usual, England did not make the most of their possession in midfield.

Three early infringements were punished with slide-rule accuracy by Ireland's new goal-kicking wonder, Ollie Campbell.

Three goals inside seven minutes on his championship debut took the Irish fly-half's incredible streak to 16 out of 17 attempts at goal.

But even when they trailed 9-3 it was clear that England could not be denied.

After half an hour they added to Hare's seventh minute penalty with a great try by scrum-half Steve Smith.

Beaumont, winger Carleton and Smith all made charges in the frantic build-up. And the Irish were literally on their knees when Smith went again to cross the line and Hare converted.

Beaumont has never played better at international level and must now be favourite to take the British Lions to South Africa next summer.

He set up a ruck from which John Horton hoisted a high kick for Slemen to run on to and score wide out. Hare's touchline conversion sailed over.

Luckily for the Irish, England never found the punch or rhythm in rhythm in midfield that they possessed up front.

Feeding on scraps, Ireland's backs were far more enterprising, even after they lost Mc-Naughton in the first half with a leg injury.

INJURED

England also lost fierce - tackling centre Tony Bond midway through the second half with a suspected bro-

So, the policy of half-backs Smith and Horton was understandably to keep the ball in front of Beaumont's driving forwards.

It was pressure that brought a second penalty for Hare and nearly produced tries for Smith and Beaumont.

But it wasn't until the seventh minute of injury time that John Scott gathered from the back of a scrum and raced 20 yards to the line unopposed.

Hare 8	O'Brien 6
Carleton 8	Kennedy 7
Bond 7	McKibbin 7
Preston 7	McNaughton (inj) 7
Slemen 8	McLennan 8
J. Horton 7	Campbell 8
Smith 8	Patterson 8
Cotton 8	Orr 5
Wheeler 8	Fitzgerald 6
Blakeway 8	McLouglin 6
*BEAUMONT 9	Keane 7
N. Horton 8	Glennon 6
Uttley 8	O'Driscoll 7
Neary 8	*SLATTERY 9
Scott 8.	Duggan 7.
Sub : Woodward	Sub: Burns 7

Ref: C. Thomas (Wales) 8.

FULL-POWER ENGLAND THE TOPS

ENGLAND'S hopes for a successful season soared like the price of gold bullion with their crushing victory over Ireland at Twickenham.

Not since England won 16—0 in 1962 have they so comprehensively hammered the Irish.

Skipper Billy Beaumont said before the game that his side was fed up with failure.

Well, there was no failure here. Ireland, fancying their Triple Crown chances after their successes in Australia during the summer, were demoralised by three tries, and Beaumont nearly made it a fourth when he was over the Irish line but was held up.

Penalty

Ireland actually led 9—3 by the 22nd minute — thanks to the immaculate kicking of their potential match-winner fly-half Ollie Campbell, who slotted three penalty goals with superb nonchalance in reply to England full-back Dusty Hare's first penalty goal of the match.

But nerves were stretched as taut as violin strings in

England 24, Ireland 9

defence and under English forward pressure they cracked.

England stormed to their line. Both Beaumont and scrum-half Steve Smith were stopped before Smith dived over in triumph. Hare converted, and England were level.

Then came a dreadful error that changed the course of the game for Ireland.

Keven O'Brien, the Lancashire full-back who opted for Ireland rather than rely on his English qualifications, tried to hack clear a long Smith punt, missed the ball completely and left-wing Mike Slemen snapped it up eagerly to score. It was a gift try that shattered Ireland.

Poor O'Brien went from bad to worse, was always suspect under the high ball and his first cap may well be his last. I can imagine the Lancashire lads in the England side were well aware of his weaknesses.

However, it was really the big, powerful England pack that destroyed the lighter Irish. And new tight head prop Phil Blakeway can be well satisfied with his solid contribution to the front row platform.

England outpushed the Irish forwards in the loose scrums, won the rucks and mauls, and smashed them in the line-outs. Nigel Horton, recalled when Maurice Colclough withdrew through injury, was a major force in England's 25—15 winning line-out margin.

Beaumont's charges in the loose, the tight control of the packs from front to back and the strength of the English back row in which Roger Uttley made a distinguished reappearance—as a flanker—and their combined mastery of the Irish forwards helped their confidence blossom like red roses.

With such superiority, the England half-backs Steve Smith

and John Horton, although starting nervously, also bloomed. Both had their best games to date.

Smith's kicking in support of his pack's was accuracy itself and Horton's authority grew visibly.

He hoisted high kicks with great effect and began to run at the Irish defence. For the first time at International level he reproduced his Bath club form.

England had the promise to expand their game and once in control did just that.

Unhappily, they lost centre Tony Bond with a fractured right leg in the second half after he had made a terrific tackle on Irish centre Alistair McKibbin. Leicester centre Clive Woodward came on as replacement for his first cap.

Bond was later operated on at West Middlesex hospital and he will be out for the rest of the season.

With Dusty Hare in good kicking form with three conversions and a penalty, England's bounce and mastery was finally completed in injury time straight from a five-yard scrum when No. 8 John Scott, carrying the ball in one hand, bulldozed over for England's third try.

Nippy

Strangely, disappointing Ireland looked more threatening when they, too, tried to run the ball. Big lock Moss Keane tried in vain to break down the tenacious English defence and their nippy scrum half Colin Patterson was magnificent in tidying up their mistakes. But this was England's day.

Chairman of the selectors Budge Rogers said: "That was the best England performance for a long time. The scrummaging was superb."

CLEAR . . . Ireland's Colin Patterson passes as England's Steve Smith moves in to tackle

England turn on a rare

Follow me . . . Slemen shows Smith the way, but Orr cannot keep track of him and the England wing is away on the run

super-show

It's King Billy !

by Norman Harris

ENGLAND can do it and they have ! Their victory against Ireland at Twickenham yesterday was more impressive than any of their rare successes in recent years, for this time they beat a side that frequently demonstrated match-winning potential. Indeed, England were behind by 3-9 and had to overcome a crisis of confidence. They did so spectacularly.

Overall, the match was exciting beyond most people's expectation, though not all Irishmen may think so. England made one of their best and, certainly, most entertaining starts but very soon their opening penalty was cancelled with interest as Campbell, three times in three attempts, put the ball between the posts.

After Campbell's three hammer blows, which flaunted England's ball-winning superiority throughout this period, the men in white seemed to be once again losing their composure, especially around the fringes of their forward possession.

Then, the balance on the scoreboard again changed dramatically. An inroad to the corner by Horton and Hare led to a period of intense pressure on the Irish line. The efforts looked a little too frenetic, but the Irishmen were evidently so pulled around that when the ball popped up for Smith there was a hole such as must have made him pinch himself as he claimed a try.

Smith was again to the forefront as he ran on the blind side, then kicked instead of passing. Slemen must have been close to a half-yard offside as he chased into the corner, but his try, as O'Brien's fly-hack failed, was well merited reward for this excellent servant of England in attack and defence.

Both Hare's conversions succeeded and the re-start saw England in almost euphoric command. From their own line, Slemen's slamming touch kick, from Smith's long, calm pass, then Horton using midfield possession to torpedo the ball into the corner, put England right back where they wanted to be.

And immediately after the resumption, England surged down the blind side and over the line. A number of pressure scrums followed and Smith was so certain he had scored after Ireland raked the ball and lost control in goal, and could not understand the scrum being reconvened, he was very nearly guilty of grabbing the referee. Reward, which by now England seems to expect, came with a Hare penalty.

For a period, Ireland were almost back on terms and within a whisker of a memorable try. In the finest movement of the match their backs snapped into action from opportunist possession and the ball was as smartly returned through many hands but went forward on the line.

This moment apart, England began to coast to victory. For once, they had men playing well in key positions. Hare at full back and Smith at scrum half had their best internationals and Horton for once looked an effective player at this level. Bond charged effectively, until his sad departure by stretcher, and Beaumont led the forwards in following up with more hard pounding.

It must be many a day since an Irish pack has absorbed such punishment. Not that they cracked, but it surely sapped them Towards the end they were going back *en bloc* and when, in the last seconds, Scott picked up from a scrum, there was scarcely an arm raised to stop him galloping through to the line.

England: W. Hare (Leicester); J. Carleton (Ovvell), A. Bond (Sale), N. J. Preston (Richmond), M. Slemen (Liverpool); J. Horton (Bath), S. Smith (Sale); No. 8, J. Scott (Cardiff; Second Row, A. Neary (Broughton Park), N. Horton (Moseley), W. Beaumont (Fylde, capt.), R. Uttley (Wasps); Front Row, P. Blakeway (Gloucester), P. Wheeler (Leicester), F. Cotton (Sale).

Replacement: C. Woodward (Leicester) for Bond.

Tries: Smith, Slemen, Scott. **Conversions:** Hare (3). **Penalty goals:** Hare (2).

IRELAND: K. O'Brien (Broughton Park); T. Kennedy (St Mary's Coll), A. McKibbin (L. Irish), P. McNaughton (Greystones), A. McLennan (Wanderers); O. Campbell (O. Belvedere), C. Patterson (Instonians); No. 8, W. Duggan (Blackrock Coll); Second Row, F. Slattery (Blackrock, capt), J. Glennon (Skerries), M. Keane (Lansdowne), J. O'Driscoll (L. Irish); Front Row, G. McLoughlin (Shannon), C. FitzGerald (St Marys), P. Orr (O.Wesley).

Replacement: I. Burns (Wanders) for McNaughton.

Penalty goals: Campbell (3).

REFEREE: C. Thomas (Wales).

WELL HELD ... Irish forward Willie Duggan wraps a tackle round Steve Smith's legs. Horton and Cotton move in to help.

CHAMPIONSHIP TABLE	P	W	D	L	F	A	Pts
England ..	1	1	0	0	24	9	2
Wales	1	1	0	0	18	9	2
France	1	0	0	1	9	18	0
Ireland ...	1	0	0	1	9	24	0
Scotland ..	0	0	0	0	0	0	0

FEBRUARY 2 1980

1980 FIVE NATIONS: ENGLAND ENJOY VICTORY OVER FRANCE IN PARIS

WINNING PACK!

Billy's tornados humiliate France

FRANCE . . . 13   ENGLAND . . . 17

ENGLAND recovered brilliantly from a disastrous start to destroy France in a thriller at the Parc des Princes, Paris.

It was England's finest day on the rugby field in years and throws wide open this season's Five Nations championship.

And it was the English pack that assured victory with a superb performance. As the Welsh forwards succeeded at the Arms Park a fortnight ago, so England's magnificent eight dominated yesterday with a similar show of controlled strength.

HOW THEY STAND

	P	W	L	F	A	Pts
ENGLAND	2	2	0	41	22	4
WALES	1	1	0	18	9	2
IRELAND	2	1	1	31	39	2
SCOTLAND ...	1	0	0	15	22	0
FRANCE	2	0	0	22	35	0

HANDS UP

□ COLCLOUGH reaches high for a ball in a line-out as England battle towards victory.

Rare sight in Paris; France attacking with Duhard in the van

FRENCH LESSON!

England, our England

| France | 13pts |
| England | 17pts |

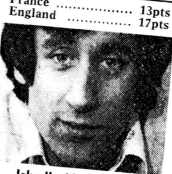

John Hopkins reports from Paris

THERE weren't many stiff upper lips in Paris last night. Earlier England had just ended a 16-year run without victory in the French capital by crushing a poor French side for 40 minutes, and then inflicting a Chinese torture on their own loyal supporters by almost allowing the home side to snatch a draw or, horror of horrors, victory, in the last exciting minutes.

All round the Madeleine, near the team's hotel in the Gare St. Lazare, wherever you looked in fact, the men in their blazers and gleaming buttons walked, laughed and joked away their pent-up emotions. They had seen England win at last! and even the meanest Frenchman must doff his beret to the English forwards, who grabbed victory for their team with a display of such awesome power that spectators were left hushed.

From mid-way through the first half to mid-way through the second, England's forwards, with more than 150 caps between them, almost toyed with the inexperienced French. They won rucks and mauls, they drove from line-outs and scrums, they probed the blind-side unceasingly, never really varying from their basic tune of forward superiority. They were so strong that even when Roger Uttley had to leave the field briefly with a bloody face, his seven colleagues held the French drive at a scrum to allow John Horton the time to land a successful dropped goal.

By the second turning point, which marked the start of the French revival, England had scored two tries and Horton had added a second dropped goal. The score had thus changed in England's favour from 3-7 to 17-7.

For 22 minutes in the second half the French could mount only one serious attack which ended when their left wing Jean-Luc Averous was stopped 20 yards out.

At 7-7 only a forward pass from the captain Bill Beaumont to right wing John Carleton prevented a try. Outside, Clive Woodward in particular with his snaky runs often brought the ball back to England's all-conquering forwards. An exception was when he slipped it on to Nick Preston and the rangy centre shook off two tackles in his successful 20 yard dash to the line.

But the sheer physical effort inevitably took its toll and France, prompted by the worried-looking Jean-Pierre Rives, at last got back into the game, typically with a thundering move that began at a line-out and ended only 20 yards from England's line with a desperate tackle on Averous. Now it was England's turn to face the storm. France chose to run a penalty ten yards from England's line when they trailed by 10 points and their nippy scrumhalf Jerome Gallion was just stopped on the line. Moments later Patrick Salas knocked on under the post. Against the head France won the scrum, Averous outpaced Carleton for a try, and Alain Caussade's conversion took the score to 13-17.

France had one more shot in their locker and for what must have seemed an age for every Englishman in the stand, they attacked from deep in their own half. At least half the team handled before England somehow bundled Averous into touch 10 yards out. Before the line-out started there was scarcely an Englishman with the strength to stand up straight. But they held on and Horton nervously kicked the ball into touch to end the game.

FRANCE: S. Gabernet (Toulouse); D. Bustaffa (Carcassonne), R. Bertranne (Bagneres), D. Codorniou (Narbonne), J-L. Averous (La Voulte); A. Caussade (Lourdes), J. Gallion (Toulon). No 8: M. Carpentier (Lourdes). Second Row: J-L. Joinel (Brive), A. Maleig (Oloron), Y. Duhard (Bagneres). Front Row: J-P. Rives (Toulouse), capt; R. Paparemborde (Pau), P. Dintrans (Tarbes), P. Salas (Narbonne). **Tries:** Rives, Averous. **Conversion:** Caussade. **Penalty goal:** Caussade.

ENGLAND: W. M. Hare (Leicester); J. Carleton (Orrell), C. R. Woodward (Leicester), N. J. Preston (Richmond), M. A. C. Slemen (Liverpool); A. Horton (Bath), S. J. Smith (Sale); No 8: J. P. Scott (Cardiff); Second Row: A. Neary (Broughton Park), M. J. Colclough (Angouleme), W. B. Beaumont (Fylde), capt; R. J. Uttley (Wasps); Front Row: P. J. Blakeway (Gloucester), P. J. Wheeler (Leicester), F. E. Cotton (Sale). **Tries:** Preston, Carleton. **Penalty goal:** Hare. **Droped goals:** Horton (2). **Referee:** C. Norling (Wales).

Horton's drop of bubbly

CLEM THOMAS in Paris

FRANCE	13 pts
ENGLAND	17 pts

ENGLAND yesterday won their first game at Parc de Princes and confirmed that at last they are on a new path which can take them to the Championship which has eluded them since 1963.

Nobody can deny that they earned the best champagne in France which victory by an penalty goal and two tries to a goal and a penalty goal and a try entitled them to.

England's last win in Paris was in 1964 at Stade Colombes and perhaps it is not without significance that on that occasion the side included the new chairman of selectors, Budge Rogers, and their new coach, Mike Davis.

This time they came to prove that their pack were possibly the best in the Championship and, apart from their aberrations in the last 10 minutes, when the French were in charge, they did exactly that as their hard-driving physical presence destroyed a strangely non-combative French pack.

Experience was on England's side. They had 149 caps in their pack opposed by only 78 by the French. While six England forwards were in double figures, only Rives and Paparemborde were equally qualified.

Again, scrummaging was the decisive factor. Although France took the only strike against the head, from which they scored, the England front row broke the French morale up front. Blakeway proved a true son of Gloucester, and Wheeler and Cotton made the point that they were true British Lions, backed by the honesty and endeavours of Beaumont and Colclough in the second row.

Such a solid foundation allowed the back row to employ their defensive and attacking arts to the full. Here Neary was at his best on his forty-first appearance for England, which takes him level with Noel Murphy, of Ireland, as the most capped British flanker.

There was evidence, too, that the English half-backs had found a silver lining. Smith, in particular, played a decisive hand in affairs. And Horton's positive kicking contribution included two invaluable and well-taken dropped goals.

There was another ray of hope in the England mid-field, where Woodward looks to have the ability to mature into a fine centre. If there was a criticism of the England midfield, it was it was that they failed to read the bunching defence of the French midfield. The situation, especially in the first half, screamed for long passes to create the overlap. Unhappily, they never materialised.

Considerable criticism can be levelled at the French selectors who, faced with problems at prop, second row and No. 8, played Russian roulette by again selecting an inexperienced prop such as Salas and a young and obviously immature No. 8, even if his name was Carpentier.

Apart from the first five and the last 10 minutes, the French were never able to employ the undoubted quality and flair of their backs. Consequently, French hopes are in ruins. The crucial match will be that between England and Wales at Twickenham in two weeks' time.

After a wet, windy morning the clouds cleared to bring sunshine at the kick-off. France's first threat was a high kick to the England posts which Hare coolly disposed of by taking a difficult catch a foot behind his own line to minor. After the drop-outs, a long England kick was gathered by Gabarnet, the new French full back, who hoisted the ball back into the England half, where France won the ball at an embryo loose ruck. Gallion rapidly put the ball away to Caussade ; Bertranne cut sharply for the English line and, when held, slipped the ball

CHAMPIONSHIP TABLE

	P.	W.	D.	L.	F.	A.	Pts.
England	2	2	0	0	41	22	4
Wales	1	1	0	0	18	9	2
Ireland	2	1	0	1	31	39	2
Scotland	1	0	0	1	15	22	0
France	2	0	0	0	22	35	0

again to Gallion, who put Rives over for an ominously fast and easy French try after only three minutes. This was a great setback to English morale.

The England forwards rapidly buckled down to the task of winning possession. A brave break by Smith and a grubber kick by the scrum-half to the narrow side gave England a platform from which they were awarded a penalty from the line-out, where the French backs were offside. Hare kicked a neat penalty. Disastrously, this relief was shortlived, and dissipated when a minute later France were penalised for collapsing a scrum. Cotton, seemingly with an assault on Paparemborde, caused the referee to reverse his decision and Caussade kicked the penalty.

The England pack continued to be impressive physically, taking on the far looser French forwards. England developed attacks which were abortive because too many passes were spilt. But England clicked when, from a neat chip by Horton, the forwards quickly won a ruck. Smith and Horton moved the ball speedily for Woodward to make a quick thrust before giving to Preston, who with Slemen outside him, dangerously elected to take on a halfhearted tackle by Codorniou but managed to go over for a try to level the score.

The French were now firmly on their heels. England were confident and imposing great authority and pressure. They took the lead after a strong drive in the loose, initiated by Scott, was taken on by Smith and Beaumont and Smith again. The scrum-half fed Carleton who got over in the corner.

Some mighty scrummaging, reminiscent of the Lions in South Africa in 1974, began to break up the French pack. With English pressure remorseless, there came a brave charge through the middle by Carleton which, although wrecked on a French tackle, saw Woodward gaining possession and throwing an intelligent ball to Horton. With oodles of room he sweetly dropped a goal to put England into an emphatic 14—7 lead at halftime.

Immediately after the interval the English forwards improved as rapidly as the price of bullion. Woodward embarked on another of his snaky runs, which took him back into the sticky web of the forwards. England won the ruck for Horton to drop another priceless goal.

The danger of allowing the French any loose aopportunity became apparent when Cordoniou, from a cool move, smashed his way to within a yard of the line. Then Gallion almost got over from a short penalty. For the first time since the opening stages, England were under threat as Rives and Salas threw their talents into another attack to the English posts.

French pressure was rewarded when they won a strike against the head under the England posts. Gallion worked the ball left for Caussade to win the overlap and put Averous over in the corner for a try, which Caussade converted brilliantly from the touchline to bring the French into the nerve-racking position of only being one score in arrears.

This victory devalues the the Welsh win over the French at Cardiff, so the scene is dramatically set for the match against Wales at Twickenham. Wales must be wary of an England pack who will be a different proposition to the far less combative French pack they overwhelmed in Cardiff.

France . Tries—J-P Rives, J-L Averous. **Conversion**—A Caussade. **Penalty goal**—Caussade. **England : Tries**—N Preston, J Carleton. **Penalty goal**—W Hare. **Dropped goals**—J Horton (2).

FRANCE : S Gabernet (Toulouse) D Bustaffa (Carcassonne), R Bertranne (Bagneres), D Codorniou (Narbonne), J-L Averous (La Voulte) ; A Caussade (Lourdes), J Gallion (Toulon) ; R Paparemborde (Tarbes) P Dintrans (Pau), P Salas (Narbonne), Y Dubart (Bagneres), A Maleig (Oloron), J-L Joinel (Brives), M Carpentier (Lourdes) J-P Rives (Toulouse, captain).

ENGLAND : W H Hare (Leicester) J Carleton (Orrell), N J Preston (Richmond), C R Woodward (Leicester), M A C Slemen (Liverpool) ; J P Horton (Bath), S J Smith (Sale) ; P J Blakeway (Gloucester), P J Wheeler (Leicester), F E Cotton (Sale), M J Colclough (Angouleme), W B Beaumont (Fylde captain), R M Uttley (Wasps), J T Scott (Cardiff), A Neary (Broughton Park).

Stand-offish : Horton, the man who kicked the French all over the Parc, hands it out.

1980 FIVE NATIONS: ENGLAND BEAT WALES WITH LAST-MINUTE PENALTY

The battle of

A HARE'S

Ringer on

THE steely nerve of full back Dusty Hare hoisted Billy Beaumont's Englishmen to the brink of a Grand Slam to open the 1980s—and gave them only their fourth win against Wales at Twickenham since the war.

RUGBY TABLE

	P	W	D	L	Pts
ENGLAND	3	3	0	0	6
IRELAND	2	1	0	1	2
WALES	2	1	0	1	2
SCOTLAND	2	1	0	1	2
FRANCE	3	0	0	3	0

■ OFF! Referee David Burnett gives the "get marching" order to Wales's Paul Ringer after a high tackle against victorious England at Twickenham.

Twickenham BREADTH!
trial today

SHAME OF RINGER AS ENGLAND GRAB GLORY

TWICKENHAM trembled. English hearts pounded like drums. Then, in the first minute of injury time, full-back Dusty Hare kicked a 26-yard penalty from out near the touchline, the ball curved between the posts—and England had won a dramatic, pulsating victory.

Excited English supporters, starved of success for so long, swirled on to the pitch to acclaim Billy Beaumont's side as if they had already won the Triple Crown and Five Nations Championship for the first time since 1963. Now they should—if they defeat Scotland at Murrayfield next month.

But their moment of glory cannot wipe out the distasteful memory of Welsh flanker Paul Ringer being sent off by Irish referee Dave Burnett in the 15th minute for elbowing John Horton after the England fly half had holsted a high punt.

It soured the match. Ringer, who had been accused by television of rough play in the Wales-France game at Cardiff, walked off his head bowed, his arms on his hips —a dismal picture of dejection and disbelief.

The first player to be dismissed at Twickenham in an international since New Zealand All Black forward Cyril Brownlee was ordered off in 1925, Ringer will now be left out of the Welsh team for the rest of the season.

The danger signs had been there right from the explosive,

by JOHN REED: England 9, Wales 8

tempestious start. The pre-match build-up, with allegations of tough play on both sides, had probably been too great and the tension spilled over like molten lava.

The aggro was obvious in the first quarter as the two packs went at each other as if it were a multi-heavyweight contest.

Referee Burnett called up both captains, Billy Beaumont and Jeff Squire, to issue a general warning. Then came the moment of ignomony for Ringer—and Hare kicked the penalty that put England in front.

The golden year of Wales, chasing their fifth successive Triple Crown, is over, but what a sad way for it to end.

To their eternal credit, the 14 Welshmen responded nobly. The seven-man pack was magnificent in holding Beau-

mont's eight, none more so than skipper Squires himself, who did the work of two men in stopping England attacking on both sides of the scrum.

Wales still looked the more skilful, better balanced team. Scrum half Terry Holmes became an eighth forward in defence in defying the English pressure and fending off Steve Smith. Fly half Gareth Davies's tactical touch kicking was superb. And their backs were still prepared to run the ball.

Despite their heavy handicap, they even took the lead in the 17th minute. England heeled over their own line, scrum half Smith failed to pick up the ball and Squire, with the swiftness of a poacher, dived on to itto

They got a second try, too, in the closing minutes of the second half when, having resisted heroically and brilliantly all the English pressure, hooker Alan Phillips charged down Smith's kick, fed Elgan Rees with an inside pass and the rigth wing streaked over for what appeared to be the match winner.

But Welsh joy among their 10,000 supporters in the 55,000 crowd sank as low as a minshaft two minutes later when Wales were penalised in the ruck.

Roar

Hare kicked the penalty that settled it and the roar "England, England England," rose above Twickenham.

Hare had already missed two penalties inside three minutes in the second half. The first was awarded after Mike Rafter — replacement for injured flanker Roger Uttley— had been elbowed in the ribs.

Hare, however kicked a 35-yard penalty two minutes later to restore England's lead at 6—4.

He was successful altogether with three shots out of seven at goal, whereas Wales had failed to capitalise on their penalty chances which could have made the game safe for them.

This was a match which Wales lost rather than England won.

The English back could gain no ascendancy over the Welsh seven, and their backs were subdued and produced no more than a couple of combined movements in this controversial, sensational victory.

Ringer's case will be investigated today by an international sub-comittee of George Burrell (Scotland), Gwilym Treharne (Wales) and Albert Agar (England) in London.

FLARE-UP . . . Heated argument between England captain Bill Beaumont and Geoff Wheel of Wales

WELSH WAILS

HAPPY HARE!

The winner . . . Beaumont celebrates

1980 FIVE NATIONS: ENGLAND WIN GRAND SLAM FOR FIRST TIME IN 23 YEARS

Glory, Glory for Beaumont's boys

D-DAY

WILL KING BILLY LEAD THE LIONS?

BILLY'S BRAVES STORM TO GLORIOUS VICTORY

SALUTE Billy Beaumont's braves! After 23 years of frustration and often humiliating defeat England have won the lot—the Grand Slam, the Five Nations' Championship, the Triple Crown and the Calcutta Cup. They crushed Scotland before an enthralled 75,000 at Murrayfield with a five-try blitz in one of the most exciting, spectacular, running games I have ever seen.

For a jubilant England captain Beaumont, whose example has inspired England this season, and the rest of his dedicated side, it was the fulfilment of a Rugby dream and fitting reward for many players who have suffered the bitterness of past failures.

If there have been reservations about England's limitations and their concentration on 10-man

Scotland 18 England 30: by JOHN REED

rugby, it is the result that counts.

English pride is sky-high again and as Beaumont said: "We are in the history books for ever."

England's selectors, led by chairman Budge Rogers and coach Mike Davis, were also happy men.

It was England's highest score against Scotland and by half time, with the Englishmen 19—3 up, the championship had been decided.

There was no way that England were going to relax their steely grip on their first title since 1963.

England's power pack dominated the rucks and mauls, rolling forward like a white painted tank to contain and pressure the Scots.

And the Scottish defence appeared paper-thin with gaps yawning as wide as Princes Street as left centre Clive Woodward weaved and dodged his way through to set up first right-wing John Carleton and then left-wing Mike Slemen for tries which full-back Dusty Hare converted.

Then came another killer blow initiated by the England pack. A five-yard England scrum saw No 8 John Scott and scrum-half Steve Smith combine on the short side to send Carleton over again.

The English pattern was the same which had defeated the

FINAL TABLE

	P	W	D	L	F	A	Pts
England	4	4	0	0	80	48	8
Ireland	4	2	0	2	70	65	4
Wales	4	2	0	2	50	45	4
France	4	1	0	3	55	75	2

other countries. Tight, disciplined forward control backed by consistent half-back kicking.

Then they capitalised on Scottish mistakes with Woodward creating openings and Carleton completing a hat-trick of tries with such elusiveness, energy and appetite that they must have made sure of places on the British Lions tour of South Africa.

To their eternal credit the Scots, beaten forward and restricted in possession, rallied brilliantly in the second half. Their adventurous backs, forced to attack from deep positions, stretching the game into a marvellous contest.

As Beaumont said afterwards: "They allowed us to play some rugby, too." The pace was exhausting, the atmosphere electric.

Full back Andy Irvine, who had a nightmarish first half full of errors. Jim Renwick and fly-half John Rutherford produced some magic running that needed all England's determination to contain.

Grounded

Although Steve Smith slipped over for England's fourth try, Scotland continued to attack. Renwick zig zagged through the English defence and although grounded, lock Alan Tomes was up to score.

And after Carleton's third try, Scotland enraptured their supporters with a brilliant swerving run by fly-half John Rutherford for a score under the post.

However no one can deny that England deserve their triumph. It was a memorable moment, not least for flanker Tony Neary winning a record 43rd England cap, Fran Cotton, winning his 30th, and Beaumont who has led England to this great triumph.

SCOTLAND.—Tries: Tomes, Rutherford. Pen goals: Irvine (2). Conversions: Irvine (2).

ENGLAND.—Tries: Carleton (3), Slemen, Smith. Pen goals: Hare (2). Conversions: Hare (2).

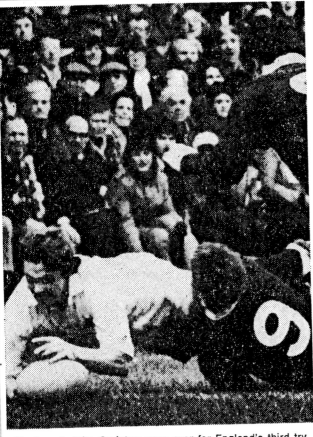

It's there! John Carleton goes over for England's third try

Scotland 18pts, England 30

After 23 aching years, England win the lot

| Scotland .... 18 pts | England .... 30 pts |

by John Hopkins

EVEN the most curmudgeonly Scotsman of all—the most Micawberish type — could scarcely begrudge England the Grand Slam, the International Championship, the Triple Crown and the Calcutta Cup after a game in which Scotland played a full part to make it one of the most memorable of recent internationals.

There were seven tries in the highest-scoring game ever between the two old rivals, and England got five of them, as many as they had scored in their three previous matches this season. That was sufficient to give them their eighth Grand Slam, their 15th Triple Crown, and their 18th Championship and, just to round off the facts and figures, for them to record their highest score against Scotland in over 100 years, exceeding their 27—14 victory in 1967.

Yet the jaunty mood of the Scots spectators as they hurried away from grey old Murrayfield was in itself a salute to their own team, which rallied in the second half to probe and dart and time and again take the capacity crowd to the edge of their seats.

At times, Scotland played Barbarian rugby, the sort the famous touring team produced in the easier games on their Easter tour. The Scots were anxious to reduce the 16-point deficit they faced at half-time, and desperate to try and reproduce the astonishing comeback they had made when they had scored 18 points in 13 minutes on the same ground a month ago.

But that was against the French. This time they could score only 15 in 29 minutes, and that wasn't enough.

For minutes after the game, supporters stood five deep outside England's changing room, chanting incantations to Beaumont. In his 13th game as captain, big Bill must have clinched his place as captain of the Lions, and helped his friends Tony Neary, England's most capped player, and Fran Cotton, England's most capped prop forward, to celebrate their individual achievements.

For most of the first half, England had enormous forward dominance, reminiscent of that 30 minutes against the French in Paris. They drove the straggly Scots back and back in the scrums, allowing John Horton to probe unerringly with his right-footed kicks.

After 30 minutes had gone, England had scored three tries. It was the Ides of March, and a slaughter was imminent. All three tries came from set pieces — who says there isn't much on from set-piece play these days? —two from England's line-outs, one from an England scrum. John Carleton got the first try after a break in midfield, and also the third when England's forwards had pushed their way almost to the Scottish line before Scott picked up and passed quickly to Smith, who flicked it on to the right wing.

Hectic would not be a strong enough word to describe the second half as play got faster and faster. The Scots were committed to all-out attack, but each time they scored England replied immediately. Renwick, Johnston and Rutherford were an electric trio in midfield, and Robertson and Irvine were just as dangerous. Twice the elusiveness of Renwick either set up a try or made the initial indentation from

which a try was scored. And inspired by their three-quarters, Beattie, a raw yet extremely promising No. 8, and even soft Alan Tomes showed flashes of genuine belligerence.

The trouble for Scotland was that after they had pulled back to 12-23 Dusty Hare kicked a quick penalty and then Carleton scored his third try of the afternoon after some sloppy fielding by Irvine. With 11 minutes remaining, Rutherford carved through after the giant David Gray had thrown back a pass from a maul on England's line. Irvine's conversion made the score 18-30.

Johnston was nearly through before Woodward caught him; Irvine and John Gossman, replacing Bruce Hay, nearly broke clear in midfield, and then Renwick picked the ball up brilliantly and launched Johnston at England's line again.

But it was all too late. That 16-point lead England took in the first half was as sound a defence as they could have wanted against the Scottish attacks of the second half.

SCOTLAND.—A. Irvine (Heriot's FP. capt); K. Robertson (Melrose), J. Renwick (Hawick), D. Johnston (Watsonians), B. Hay (Boroughmuir); J. Rutherford (Selkirk), R. Laidlaw (Jedforest); No 8: J. Beattie (Glasgow Academicals); Second row: M. Biggar (London Scottish), D. Gray (West of Scotland), A. Tomes (Hawick), D. Leslie (Gala); Front row: N. Rowan (Boroughmuir), K. Lawrie (Gala), J. Burnett (Heriot's FP).
Tries: Tomes, Rutherford. Convs: Irvine 2. Pens: Irvine 2.
Replacement: J. Gossman (West of Scotland) for Hay (55).

ENGLAND.—W. Hare (Leicester); J. Carleton (Orrell), C. Woodward (Leicester), P. Dodge (Leicester), M. Slemen (Liverpool); No 8: J. Scott (Bath), S. Smith (Sale); No 8: J. Scott (Cardiff); Second row: A. Neary (Broughton Park), M. Colclough (Angouleme), W. Beaumont (Fylde, capt), R. Uttley (Wasps); Front row: P. Blakeway (Gloucester), P. Wheeler (Leicester), F. Cotton (Sale).
Tries: Carleton 3, Slemen 1, Smith 1.
Convs: Hare 2. Pens: Hare 2.
Referee: J-P Bonnet (France).

England's Uttley falls, but for Scotland's Burnett and Tomes it was only a momentary advantage

Hail Billy's brilliant braves

MARCH 15 1980

SCOTLAND BEAT ENGLAND IN CENTENARY MATCH TO TAKE CALCUTTA CUP

SCOTLAND 18 pts., ENGLAND 6 pts.

SCOTS rugby fans will remember this Centenary game as the Sale of the Century. Scotland did enough up front to win half a dozen games and they reduced England to something not far short of a rabble. But they were glad to find their visitors in such absurdly generous mood.

It was not so much a sale as a positive give-away for their ace marksman, Dusty Hare, bracketed with Ollie Campbell as the most feared place kicker in the business, managed to miss six out of eight penalties.

Not only that but Woodward and Cusworth both missed drops which their fans would normally expect them to get with their eyes shut.

The malaise among England's marksmen did not take anything away from a solid Scots win in which the operative words were graft and drive.

The pack, after one ominous push when it seemed that the hefty English eight might grind their way to an unspectacular victory, took the game by the throat and comprehensively depleted their opponents.

For much of the time it was ruck and maul and the Scottish rucking played to the recipe of their coach, Jim Telfer, carried the day.

For the rest, the Scots played it sensibly and without frills. They were a bit expensive in penalties and if Hare had been on form they could have lost the match.

But Scotland pressured England all the way through, harried them into errors of tactics and judgment, and gobbled up the chances when they came.

For Jim Aitken, the prop, the saga of his captaincy goes on and on. Four games now without a defeat—a win in Wales, two wins over England and a draw against the All Blacks.

They Said . . .

● Scotland's captain, Jim Aitken, said, "Kennedy's try just after the interval came at exactly the right time. I felt that England could not adapt their game. After a while, they became predictable, and it was just a question of knocking them down."

England captain, Peter Wheeler: "It was just one of those days for Dusty Hare. Normally, he gets the vast majority of kicks over. The conditions required primary possession delivered quickly and cleanly, and a high ratio of goals kicked. We did not manage either.

"It was impossible to move the slippery ball slickly across the field, and when we kept it close the second wave of support arrived too late."

The Triple Crown is surely well within reach in Dublin after an interval of 46 years. And following that, why not the Grand Slam at Murrayfield against France in a grand finale?

	P.	W.	L.	F.	A.	Pts.
Scotland ...	2	2	0	33	15	4
France	1	1	0	25	12	2
Wales	2	1	1	27	24	2
England ...	1	0	1	6	18	0
Ireland ...	2	0	2	21	43	0

Note, too, how Jim Pollock, coming on as a replacement for the try scorer Euan Kennedy, maintained his personal record of never playing in a beaten Scots XV.

The backs were hardly used except in chase and tackle. But, my, how they chased and how they tackled.

Baird was launched into orbit like an Exocet or so it must have seemed to the English full-back as the Scots wing regularly homed in on him as he took the ball.

Apart from the tremendous pack, I thought that the architect of this famous win was the stand off Rutherford. His line kicking was lethal, giving the defence no chance at all.

Yet he still teased the English mercilessly by putting the ball into empty spaces or putting in that little chip when everybody expected him to slam the ball to the corner.

Laidlaw, now on the fringe

CROWN IT NOW, SCOTLAND

of being Scotland's most capped scrum half, turned in yet another great performance, taking the pressure off his partner and maintaining the momentum of the attack.

Dods was hardly in any sort of trouble at full-back and he certainly showed the place kicking composure which eluded Hare.

Delight

In a pack which moved as one man, and were far livelier than the lugubrious English, we saw again the delightful understanding between Leslie and Calder at the tail of the lineout; the pressing drive of Paxton, Milne and Cuthbertson; the searing surge of Deans, a hooker extraordinary in the loose; and the vastly improved display of Tomes in the middle of the line.

For England, it must be back to the drawing-board. Their's was a pedestrian team, slack passes everywhere, and with scarcely an idea beyond the kick ahead.

How a country of their size could waste so much talent is beyond me.

Youngs and Cusworth had to wait interminably for the slow heel, but neither possessed the acceleration to worry the defence.

Their three-quarters were scarcely given a run, and Hare's troubles in kicking were bounded by some uncharacteristic error in covering the ball.

Scotland's first try, on the half-hour, was sparked by Laidlaw, carried on by Paxton, and finished off by Johnston, who sped over after a fly kick for a touchdown. Dods converted.

Hare at last got his goal-kicking together with a penalty on the stroke of half-time. Cuthbertson went off injured at the interval and was replaced by the athletic Beattie, whose arrival in the second row did not weaken the forward effort in the least.

Jubilant

Scotland scored almost at once. Rutherford scooped up a pass from Laidlaw which fell almost at his feet, deceived the defence with a shrug of his shoulders and put Kennedy over on the burst. Dods converted.

It took Hare two minutes to knock in his second penalty but he had no more joy after that and missed two more within his usual range.

Meanwhile, Dods carefully kicked one and then another to put the Calcutta Cup, the Triple Crown, and the Grand Slam beyond England's reach.

Not a bad way to celebrate a centenary by an even more commanding margin than at Raeburn Place all those long years ago.

Cuthbertson has a groin injury and Kennedy sustained a ligament knock below the knee.

Jubilant Scots skipper, Jim Aitken, felt the game was won when Scotland snatched their second try just after the interval. A vital time to score, he said, immediately after they had lost Cuthbertson.

Crowd—63,000.

Scotland — P. W. Dods; K. W. Robertson, D. I. Johnston, A. E. Kennedy (J. Pollock), G. R. T. Baird; J. Y. Rutherford, R. J. Laidlaw, J. Aitken (capt.), C. I. Deans, I. G. Milne, W. Cuthbertson (J. Beattie), A. J. Tomes, J. Calder, I. A. M. Paxton, D. C. Leslie.

England— W. H. Hare; J. Carleton, C. R. Woodward, G. H. Davies, M. A. C. Slemen; L. Cusworth, N. G. Youngs; C. S. Pearce, P. J. Wheeler (capt.), C. White, M. J. Colclough, S. Bainbridge, P. D. Simpson, J. P. Scott, P. J. Winterbottom (J. Hall).

Scotland's second jewel in the crown

ENGLAND GO SLIDING

WOE FOR WHEELER

Scotland 18pts
England 6

JIM AITKEN'S supercharged Scots are all set up for their first Triple Crown triumph in 46 years.

After drilling England into an embarrassing defeat at Murrayfield, they go to Dublin on March 3 with a great chance of becoming the kings of British rugby for only the second time.

The Scots broke a bad spell against their oldest Rugby enemy, beating them in Edinburgh for the first time since 1976. And a jubilant Aitken said afterwards: " Scotland won the first ever international in 1871. It's great that we've won the 100th too!"

England were still battling away and seemed to be well in the game when they trailed only 6-3 at half-time.

But Aitken's inspired Blue Devil's knocked them right out of the match with a crushing nine-points burst straight after the interval.

First one of Scotland's special heroes, scrum-half Roy Laidlaw, put in a high, hanging, blind-side kick that took play close to England's line.

Leicester full-back Dusty

TABLE

	P	W	L	F	A	Pts
Scotland	2	2	0	33	15	4
France	1	1	0	25	12	2
Wales	2	1	1	27	24	2
England	1	0	1	6	18	0
Ireland	2	0	2	21	43	0

Hare could not make it safe and Aitken's tearaway forwards were there in a flash to win the ruck.

John Rutherford flicked the ball on to Euan Kennedy who romped through a huge gap for his first international try. Peter Dods slotted the conversion.

Hare pulled three points back with a 33-yard penalty, but, before England had time to look up at the scoreboard, Dods was landing another penalty to make it 15—6 with just five minutes of the second half gone.

England's forwards had clung on grimly in the first half but afterwards they were steamrollered out of the contest with the Scots driving and rucking magnificently.

Scotland, who scored two tries to none, had got their first touchdown when former soccer player, David Johnston, kicked through from 20 yards out and beat three confused England defenders, Hare, Woodward and Cusworth, for the touchdown.

Hare had an unhappy time, landing just two of eight penalty shots.

SCOTLAND.—Tries: Johnston, Kennedy; Conv: Dods (2); Pen: Dods (2). ENGLAND.—Pens: Hare (2).

■ENGLAND on the ball—but it was Scotland on the boil at Murrayfield.

Jim fixes England

By ROY CLARKE   Scotland 18 England 6

JIM AITKEN'S Scottish braves took England apart.

Aitken, 36, wanted to quit rugby a happy man after leading Scotland's 22-12 triumph at Twickenham a year ago.

A Jim'll Fix It campaign persuaded him to change his mind

Now, after emphatic wins over Wales and this shambles of an English team in the 100th Anglo-Scottish clash, his country are primed to win the Triple Crown for the first time since 1938

With driving rucks and mauls and domination in the lineouts, his forwards tamed the same England pack that demolished the All Blacks

Skipper Aitken said: "England couldn't change their play to adapt to the conditions. We pinned them down and it became fairly predictable in the second half."

For record-breaking full - back Hare, the match was like a horror movie. He was at fault for both Scotland tries

and he landed just two out of eight penalty shots.

Hare was sprawling in the mud as Johnston kicked through for Scotland's first try after 28 minutes.

But the game was won and lost in 10 hectic minutes at the start of the second half.

Kennedy received a rucked ball after Hare's error and found a gap in England's defence to score.

And after nine min-

utes Scotland were decisively 15-6 up as full back, Dods added a penalty to his two conversions.

SCOTLAND—tries: Johnston, Kennedy; convs: Dods 2; pens: Dods 2. ENGLAND—pens: Hare 2.

SCOTLAND: Dods 8—Robertson 7, Kennedy (in) 7J, Johnston 7, Baird 7—Rutherford 8, Laidlaw 8—Aitken 7, Deans 8, Milne 7, Cuthbertston (inj) 7, Tomes 7, Calder 8, *LESLIE 9, Paxton 8. Sub: Pollock 6, Beattie 7.

ENGLAND: Hare 5—Carleton 6, Davies 6, Woodward 6, *SLEMEN 7 — Cusworth 6, Youngs 6—White 6, Wheeler 6, Pearce 6, Colclough 6, Bainbridge 6, Simpson 5, Winterbottom (inj) 6, Scott 5.

Look out—behind you! England scrum half NICK YOUNGS, who had a praticularly miserable afternoon, about to be downed by Scots second-row forward BILL CUTHBERTSON at Murrayfield yesterday.

Wheeler's turn : England's captain seizing on a ball going Scot-free at Murrayfield.

SCOTLAND WIN CALCUTTA CUP BY RECORD MARGIN

BATTL

'We showed England how to play'

—GAVIN HASTINGS

Look here
★ ENGLAND'S Wade Dooley (No. 4) gets to grips with Scotland's Beattie.

ENGLAND'S SCOTCHING

E OF

SCOTLAND 33, ENGLAND 6

HASTINGS

HASTINGS

HOW THEY STAND

	P	W	D	L	F	A	Pts
Scotland	3	2	0	1	66	45	4
Wales	3	2	0	1	59	48	4
England	2	1	0	1	27	51	2
France	2	1	0	1	46	27	2
Ireland	2	0	0	2	21	48	0

A FANTASTIC display of aggression, wit and sheer basic speed gave Scotland a thunderous win, their biggest in history over England and one so overwhelming in so many departments. It was another triumph for Gavin Hastings, whose 21 points were the Scottish record and who played magnificently in his other duties as well. But more than that, it was a triumph for Scotland's development, for a team with athletic forwards who hammered and harried and bustled poor, static, England, into total retreat.

Elsewhere, Scotland's faithful half-back double act was operating at all its old excellence, with Rutherford and Laidlaw sniping around

Scotland 33pts
England 6pts

the scrum. Scotland's backs finally began to show as an attacking force with Duncan and Baird splendidly aggressive on the wings. You could look all night for redeeming features for England but the only parts of the game not totally blown away were the coolness of Nigel Melville and the competitiveness of Steve Brain and Peter Winterbottom.

It was Scotland who constructed the first pressure platform, this after a jumpy opening in which the further away from the ball you looked, the more action seemed to be taking place. Hastings and Andrew - at his third attempt, mind you - put over penalties, then Scotland began to operate. Gavin Hastings chipped to the corner flag and England only broke out after a superb line-out jump by Colcough and sweeping-up by Pearce. Immediately afterwards, Matt Duncan thundered through the tackles of Harrison and Huw Davies down the right wing and was smothered in the final yards; then John Rutherford put a lovely chip behind the English centres, but Jeffrey and Baird, diving for the touch down, managed to knock on in their anxiety.

However, the pressure for Scotland duly told. Hastings made it 9-3 with his second and third penalties, awarded for barging in the line-out and for a high tackle on Baird as the Scottish wing was approaching the line after a splendid Scottish back movement. There was certainly a greater fluency and invention about Scotland's game, but when the England forwards finally roused themselves it took them a long time to score again. This was chiefly because Andrew missed two more kickable penalties, although he did pull it back to 6-9. Yet if Andrew was erratic, Gavin Hastings had no such problems in the first half. He made it 12-6 at half-time with a beautiful long kick after England had illegally lowered the scrum.

England's chances of recovery were not increased when John Hall left the field to be replaced by Nigel Redman, but not even Hall could possibly have done anything about a half which began as a drubbing and ended as a massacre.

Bird and Duncan were both stopped close to the English line after surging Scottish attacks, and Duncan may well have thrown a try away when he elected to come inside Gavin Hastings with space out on his wing.

I think we can safely say that he was forgiven after 18 minutes of the second half. Beattie, Calder and Deans drove the ball away from a scrum, Laidlaw went scampering down the blind side after the second ruck and this time, Duncan stayed out on his wing, took the pass from the galloping Gavin and blasted a path through the corner. The stadium took off and remained in orbit as Hastings landed an outstanding conversion from the touchline.

Then Scotland went into warp drive. Hastings kicked another goal - his fifth - a few minutes later when Redman was offside in a maul and England were so far back on their heels that they were almost falling over. At this stage, the only visible resistance was coming from Brain and Winterbottom, but what were two men against a pride of blue. Scotland went on improving and there was still time for two outstanding and thrilling tries to seal the afternoon. John Rutherford scored after approach work involving Calder and Beattie, then some superb passing under pressure put Scott Hastings over on the right. Gavin Hastings kicked both conversions but this was hardly the shock of the afternoon. Perhaps there was even a touch of disbelief in the hugs in which the victorious Scots were enveloped on the final whistle.

SCOTLAND: G Hastings (Watsonians): M Duncan (West of Scotland). D Johnston (Watsonians). S Hastings (Watsonians). R Baird (Kelso): J Rutherford (Selkirk), R Laidlaw (Jedforest): A Brewster (Stewart's/Melville FP). C Deans (Hawick. capt). I Milne (Harlequins) A Campbell (Hawick). I Paxton (Selkirk), J Jeffrey (Kelso), J Beattie (Glasgow Academicals). F Calder (Stewart's/Melville FP)
Tries: Duncan. Rutherford. S Hastings Conversions: G Hastings (3) Penalties: G Hastings (5)
ENGLAND: H Davies (Wasps) (rep: S Barnes (Bath): S Smith (Wasps). S Halliday (Bath). J Salmon (Harlequins). M Harrison (Wakefield): R Andrew (Nottingham). N Melville (Wasps. capt), P Rendall (Wasps). S Brain (Coventry). G Pearce (Northampton), W Dooley (Preston Grasshoppers). M Colclough (Swansea). J Hall (Bath) (rep: N.Redman (Bath). G Robbins (Coventry). P Winterbottom (Headingley)
Penalties: R Andrew (2)
Referee: R Francis (New Zealand)

Scotland

Hastings hammers a record

GAVIN HASTINGS put the boot into England as Scotland careered to a record Calcutta Cup victory.

Full-back Hastings did not miss an attempt at goal as he landed five penalties and three conversions for 21 points—a Scottish international record.

Rob Andrews, the fly-half old enemy England, could do little in reply, succeeding only twice from six penalty attempts.

England had trailed only 12-6 at half-time but the Scottish pack took complete control after the break.

England lost flanker Hall (finger injury) and full-back Davies (shoulder) but it made no difference to the result.

The Scots back row of Jeffrey, Beattie and Calder took the eye both in attack and defence and were yards quicker to the breakdown.

Half backs Rutherford and Laidlaw were allowed back to their best form and after the disappointing showing in defeat at Cardiff, Scotland were irresistagle.

Effective

And apart from Harrison, who had a fine game on the left wing, nobody in the England back division could compare with a fine Scotland threequarter line.

The England pack, in the opening quarter, won the line-outs by a mile and out-scrummaged the opposition but the longer the game went on the less effective they became.

by the time full-back davies who had played superbly in defence, went off with four minutes to play, Scotland were already home and dry with three tries under their belt.

Hastings began his onslaught in the ninth minute when he kicked a fine angled penalty from 30 yards.

England attacked with force on both sides of the field before Andrews levelled the score in the 19th minute with his third shot at goal.

Scotland retaliated in style and twice went near to scoring tries before jumping into a six-point lead with two further penalties from Hastings.

England, however, regained territorial advantage but had to rely on Andrew to reduce the deficit when he was on target for this second penalty.

Hastings redressed the situation with his fourth consecutive penalty goal, this time from 45 yards and near the touchline.

Magnificent

Scotland started the second half in magnificent style to pen england back and it was no more than they deserved when Duncan latched on to a Laidlaw pass to score in the corner. Hastings converted from the touchline.

Midway through the second half Hastings kicked his fifth penalty goal to stretch his side's lead to 15 points.

Then in the final quarter Scotland scored two cracking tries through Rutherford and Scott Hastings, Gavins brother.

Gavin converted both to send Enland home facing another season of disappointment.

Scotland: *G HASTINGS 9 — Duncan 7, Johnston 7, S Hastings 7, Baird 7—Rutherford 8, Laidlaw 8—Brewster, 7, deans 7, Milne 7, Campbell 7, Paxton 7, Jeffrey 8, Beattie 8, Calder 8.

England: Davies 7—Smith 6, Halliday 6, Salmon 6, *HARRISON 8—Andrews 6, Melville 7—Rendall 6, Brain 7, Pearce 6, Dooley 6, Colclough 6, Hall 7, Robbins 6, Winterbottom 7.

hit an all-time high

NEW ZEALAND WIN FIRST RUGBY UNION WORLD CUP

GIANTS!

☐ **ALL BLACKS** front row McDowell, FitzPatrick and Drake celebrate their World Cup win over France in Auckland.

Captain Kirk

All Blacks' skipper David Kirk is on top of the world after crushing France

Kiwis take the crown

New Zealand 29pts France 9
From ALASDAIR ROSS

BLOODY marvel David Kirk ruthlessly sealed a World Cup Blackwash in Auckland last night.

New Zealand skipper Kirk set up a crushing final win as he conjured up a devastating double second-half strike to send France crashing.

The Five Nations Grand Slam champions simply couldn't find an answer to New Zealand's bone-shaking tackling and surging forward play as scrum-half Kirk called all the shots.

Captain Kirk, who needed two stitches in an eye wound, killed off the French with two inspired moments of All Black play to clinch a richly deserved World Cup triumph.

Electrifying

Kirk struck first in the 63rd minute as he popped up on the end of yet another fierce New Zealand drive. Grant Fox and Michael Jones combined to give Kirk his chance and he made no mistake hammering through two tackles to dive over in the corner to give the All Blacks a precious 19-3 lead.

Kirk, who will play for Oxford University next season, then ended any French resistance with a perfectly timed break straight from the kick-off.

He peeled off the back of the ferocious All Black pack to carve his way downfield with an electrifying burst through the heart of the French backline.

Wayne Shelford was at Kirk's back to carry on the move and cleverly tossed the ball out to John Kirwan for the flying winger to power over for his sixth World Cup try.

That was more than enough to shatter the French, and Kirk later said: "We were always in total control. We dictated the pace of the match, and even on the rare occasion that the French threatened we stopped them

"We were superbly prepared, and this is without doubt the finest New Zealand team I've known. The French could only play as well as we allowed them, and that was a true measure of the grip we had on the game."

New Zealand were in charge from the moment stand-off Fox drilled over a 14th minute drop-goal after a neat tap-penalty.

Kiwi flanker Michael Jones swooped on a loose ball to score the first try of the game after French winger Patrice Lagisquet failed to collect a charged-down Fox drop-goal attempt.

French coach Jacques Fouroux admitted: "It was difficult to play this match so soon after beating Australia. I think that was our final."

NEW ZEALAND— Tries: Jones, Kirk Kilwan. Con: Fox. Drop-goal: Fox. Pens: Fox (4).

FRANCE—Try: Berbezier. Con: Camberabero. Pen: Camberabero.

SCOTLAND AND ENGLAND IN RACE FOR GRAND SLAM – SCOTLAND ARE VICTORIOUS

Tartan torture

SCOTLAND 13
ENGLAND 7

GRAND SLAM!

ENGLAND coach Roger Uttley confessed "we blew it" after the winner-takes-all Murrayfield showdown ended in disaster yesterday.

All-conquering England, on the verge of an incredible title four-timer, were poleaxed 13-7 by a rampant Scotland who defied all the odds to claim their own place in rugby's hall of fame.

The Scots, available at 11-4 with one leading bookmaker, clinched the Calcutta Cup, Triple Crown, Grand Slam and Five Nations Championship on an afternoon of total tartan triumph.

Will Carling's England, red-hot favourites to sweep the board, went home

Uttley blasts England

empty-handed – except for a verbal rocket from their disgusted coach.

"That was our worst performance, while Scotland produced probably their best," said Uttley, who watched his side give away two costly penalties for hitting opponents.

"Our lack of control was horrendous and it proved absolutely critical because you cannot afford to give

away points by conceding penalties.

"We were very bad in that area."

It's the second year in a row that England have blown their championship chances in their final game. Last year they lost to Wales in Cardiff with the title in their grasp.

Uttley hinted that he was not impressed with the performance of New Zealand referee David Bishop.

"Perhaps we were slow to cotton on to what was allowable," he said. "But I don't want to get involved in any controversy about that."

For the Scots, hardly given a prayer of halting the English glory march, it was a day to remember.

Defiant captain David

TABLE

	P	W	D	L	F	A	Pt
Scotland	4	4	0	0	60	26	8
England	4	3	0	1	90	26	6
France	4	2	0	2	67	78	4
Ireland	3	0	0	3	22	67	0
Wales	3	0	0	3	34	76	0

Sole, carried from the field by a delighted tartan army, said: "We showed them.

"It's an unbelievable feeling after we had been written off by everybody."

And Scottish coach Ian McGeechan revealed that his heroes had used psychological warfare to sink the English.

He ordered his players to ignore the normal run on to the pitch at the start and to walk on slowly instead.

"We wanted to show England we were there to do a job and were not going to be afraid of the battle ahead," he said.

England skipper Carling swallowed his disappointment to pay tribute to Scotland for raising their game so effectively.

"They beat us fair and square," he said.

■ **NO CALCUTTA: Wade Dooley wins a line-out for England but the Scots were the real high-fliers** *Picture: HOWARD WALKER*

JOCKS AWAY! GREAT SCOT: Damian Cronin blasts by Jeremy Guscott *Picture: HOWARD WALKER*

Their cup runneth over: Scotland's victorious rugby team celebrates last night after beating England to win the Grand Slam crown

Scotland's slam as England flop

ENGLAND'S Grand Slam dreams were shattered by a blue tide of passion in another last-match blow-out at Murrayfield.

Just as at Cardiff last year, when they blew the Five Nations Championship, Will Carling's side missed the boat.

Only this time it wasn't just the title that went out of the sunken porthole.

The Grand Slam, Triple Crown, Calcutta Cup and Five Nations crown all went to unfancied Scotland in the great winner-takes-all showdown.

And how richly the Scots deserved it after exposing big doubts about just how good this England side is going to be in next year's World Cup.

Scotland, unconvincing in their three previous wins, had always insisted England had enjoyed an armchair ride this season.

Frenzied

And they were seething at the way the bookies made England a crushing 4-1 on to make a clean sweep at Murrayfield.

England manager Geoff Cooke knew exactly what that meant.

He warned his side to expect the most frenzied opening 20 minutes any of them had ever experienced.

Even he must have been amazed at how that 20 minute warning of tartan commitment stretched right into the third minute of injury time.

At least England did have the consolation of scoring their first try at Murrayfield for 10 years.

And a marvellous one it was by Jeremy Guscott before he became one of the victims of the sizzling battle as he limped off injured in the second half.

But that was no more than a scrap of comfort for an England side still short of the killer instinct.

From the very first seconds the blue shirts swarmed everywhere, forcing errors from players who had been used to total control.

Under that pressure, England's discipline, such a feature of their exciting season, cracked badly.

Jeff Probyn was penalised for stamping on Sole, Wade Dooley for a punch and there were any number of niggling incidents that fortunately came to nothing.

That ill discipline might have presented Scotland with the lead after just 56 seconds.

Mickey Skinner strayed offside at the first ruck and when he queried New Zealand referee David Bishop's decision, England were marched back 10 metres into kicking range.

Craig Chalmers, doing all the kicking instead of Gavin Hastings, sent his 40-metre penalty drifting agonisingly wide.

But the young stand-off made no mistake with a 30 metres penalty in the fifth minute when Richard Hill was penalised for delaying the put-in at a scrum.

Stamped

It sent Murrayfield wild but it was nothing to the noise that raised the roof when Chalmers kicked his second penalty when Probyn stamped on Sole.

Against such a tidal wave of early pressure, England teams of the past would have folded completely.

But this one is filled with self-belief. They rallied to turn the match into a contest worthy of its billing.

Simon Halliday was just beaten to a wretched bounce as Guscott kicked to the corner and then Guscott himself scored a breathtaking try, his seventh in six internationals.

Mike Teague drove powerfully up the middle from a scrum before moving the ball out,

Carling carved on another 20 yards to create an overlap and Guscott sold Tony Stanger with a glorious dummy to drive over. But full back Simon Hodgkinson could not convert the difficult kick.

Things looked bleak for the Scots when brilliant number eight Derek White went off injured in the 29th minute to be replaced by Derek Turnbull.

But once again, England cracked when Dooley was lectured for a wild lineout offence and Chalmers kicked the goal to earn Scotland a 9-4 half time lead.

It looked a slender lead as England had the benefit in the second half of a strong, swirling wind.

But Stanger gave them the start that they so desperately needed when he dived over after only 64 seconds after a superb run by Gavin Hastings to put Scotland 13-4 up.

England got a much-needed boost when Hodgkinson trimmed the gap to six points with a penalty as Scotland killed a ruck.

With 25 minutes left to snatch the game, England kicked repeatedly to win lineouts yards from the Scotland try line, but each nutes.

At the end, England players sank to their knees as Scotland raced into the arms of their delirious fans, having outsmarted the old enemy by saving their best to last.

SCOTLAND.– G Hastings, Stanger, S Hastings, Lineen, Tukalo, Chalmers, Armstrong, Sole (Capt.), Milne, Burnell, Gray, Cronin, Jeffrey, Calder, White.

ENGLAND.– Hodgkinson, Halliday, Carling (Capt.), Guscott, Underwood, Andrew, Hill, Rendall, Moore, Probyn, Dooley, Ackford, Skinner, Winterbottom, Teague.

■ **TARTAN TERROR: Scotland giant John Jeffries (right) muscles in to stop Jeremy Guscott** *Picture: DAVID CANNON*

1991: ENGLAND TRIUMPH OVER FRANCE TO WIN FIRST GRAND SLAM SINCE 1980

SLAM-TASTIC!

King Carling hails heroes

■ **WILL-POWERED!** Grand slam skipper Will Carling gets a lift from delighted fans

□ **BLANKETY BLANCO!** Teague (left) and Carling get to grips with Blanco

Picture: MIKE MALONEY

AIN'T WE GRAND

Carling's glory boys put slam on France

FIVE
NATIONS
RUGBY
SPECIAL

	P	W	D	L	Pt
England...	4	4	0	0	8
France......	4	3	0	1	6
Scotland..	4	2	0	2	4
Ireland......	4	0	1	3	1
Wales	4	0	1	3	1

England surge to the Slam

ENGLAND cracked open the champagne at long last yesterday – after the grandest slam of all.

Will Carling's side just clung on in a sensational finish to land their first Grand Slam for 11 years.

It was a magical game and, while England were chaired off the pitch by delighted fans, the French were in tears after scoring three tries to one only to go home empty-handed.

Rory Underwood's 27th try for England supplied

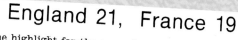
England 21, France 19

the highlight for the ecstatic home crowd and Simon Hodgkinson, who fluffed two penalties from in front of the posts, bagged 14 points and the championship record.

After losing the Grand Slam at Murrayfield last year and having the title ripped from them at Cardiff two seasons ago, England couldn't afford another slip in World Cup year.

But from 18-9 at halftime, they were rocked

by some thrilling French counter attacking which had England hanging on grimly.

And when, a minute from time, Serge Blanco emerged from his personal nightmare to send Franck Mesnel in for a brilliant try which Didier Camberabero converted from the touchline, France suddenly found themselves just two points behind.

Melted

That crisis melted even the ice-man Hodgkinson, who missed a penalty from in front of the posts 30 seconds later – his second easy miss of the day.

England got off to the ideal start when Xavier Blond strayed offside in the first attack and Hodgkinson kicked the goal after just 98 seconds.

But France hit back magnificently after Hodgkinson's second penalty flew wide in the 12th minute.

Blanco, so suspect all day under the high ball, ran from behind his own posts and Lafond, Sella and Camberabero swept the ball down the right touchline.

As the England cover cut Camberabero off, the little fly-half crosskicked for Saint-Andre to pick up and dive over for what was surely one of the greatest tries ever seen in international rugby.

For a while England were rattled. The big line-out men were unable to win ball and it

took the superb back row of Peter Winterbottom, Mike Teague and Dean Richards to settle them.

Andrew equalised with a snap drop-goal and Hodgkinson kicked England ahead with a 22nd minute penalty, only for Camberabero to pull it level again when Hodgkinson deliberately threw the ball into touch.

Then Underwood really set the game alight when Carling broke from a ruck to set up his winger beautifully, and the RAF flier celebrated equalling Tony Neary's England record 43 caps by turning Lafond inside out for a great try.

Hodgkinson converted and then broke Lescarboura's championship record 54 points with another penalty to put England 18-9 up at halftime.

Hoisted

They held that until just before the hour when Camberabero hoisted an up-and-under.

Both Carling and Richards appeared to have it covered, but the ball slipped out of their grasp and Camberabero dived on it.

Hodgkinson seemed to have put England back out of sight when Blond got offside and then pushed referee Les Peard out of the way. He was lucky to escape only with a caution and the blame for the kick that put the home team 21-13 ahead.

That seemed to be

■ **JUMP LEAD: English hands are first to line-out possession** *Picture: ROB RATHBONE*

good enough until, 90 seconds from time, Blanco popped up with a surging blind side run which ended with Jeremy Guscott hauling him down from behind.

But Blanco still managed to get his pass away to Mesnel, who found Richard Hill the sole line of defence and left him for dead with a superb feint.

Camberabero's touchline conversion brought the scores to 21-19 – but England hung on and would have won with a bit to spare but for Hodgkinson's lastminute miss.

■ **SLAM AND CLASP: Rob Andrew and Jeremy Guscott celebrate England's Twickenham triumph** *Picture: ROB RATHBONE*

1991 WORLD CUP: ENGLAND BEAT FRANCE IN QUARTER-FINAL

AGGRO

★ **YOU BEAUTY!** England's Brian Moore salutes Will Carling's late try that clinches a World Cup semi-final date with Scotland.

★ But the French didn't like it . . . not one bit. Coach Daniel Dubroca and a player were seen "attacking" referee David Bishop in the tunnel at the end of the match.

★ Dubroca allegedly also accused Bishop of cheating as French fury boiled over. France made their intentions clear from the start.

Furious French 'attack' ref as England win

★ Nigel Heslop was laid out as French skipper Serge Blanco, in his farewell game, and other Frenchmen fired punches at his head.
IRON WILL – Page 39

□ **WHACKO BLANCO!** . . . Heslop's seeing stars, above, but Brian Moore is over the moon as Carling's over the line

Ooh-la-la! England triumph in World Cup thriller

V for victory: *England's Brian Moore delights in his team's 19-10 win over France in the Rugby World Cup quarter-final yesterday. Referee attacked: page 28; match report: section 2, page 14 Photograph: Chris Smith*

Fury as England storm to glory

YOU CHEAT!

From **BRIAN MADLEY**
at Parc des Princes

FRENCH coach Daniel Dubroca was accused of attacking Kiwi ref David Bishop after England stormed to a glorious World Cup victory.

Eye witnesses saw Dubroca spit at Bishop and call him a cheat in the players' tunnel after the game.

"I saw him grab the referee by the throat," said Jeff Herdman, a former Swansea player now working for BBC Radio Wales.

"He was pulled off by four other people but as they did so he spat in Bishop's face and called him a cheat."

Dubroca denied it and said: "I went to question the referee but one of his linesmen stopped me getting to him.

France 10
England 19

White wonder: Probyn, the England forward, on the charge against the French at Parc des Princes

England storm into semi-final

Referee assaulted by French coach

HEROIC, simply heroic. After a match of thunderous intensity with vivid flashes of the best and worst which sport can offer, England are in the semi-finals of the World Cup, nursing their wounds but bursting with justifiable pride. It was a magnificent effort in which they faced down French fury on a hostile afternoon.

It was a pity the day was marred by a disgraceful scene after the match when the referee, David Bishop, was attacked in the tunnel leading to the dressing rooms by Pascal Ondarts and Daniel Dubroca, the French coach. Ondarts threw a punch at Bishop and missed, and then Dubroca joined in. Dubroca grabbed Bishop around the collar with both hands and was dragged off shouting by David Lawrence, one of the linesman. Dubroca spat at Bishop and called him a "cheat".

Bishop, a New Zealander regarded as one of the top six officials in the game, was hustled into his dressing room, visibly upset. He had given only a few controversial decisions in the game and was also manhandled by Ondarts after he had penalised him in the second half, an incident which saw England take the lead at 13-10.

Later, Dubroca tried to laugh off the incident. "It was just a fraternal gesture to a referee I have known for a long time," he said. However, a journalist who saw the affair said there was nothing friendly about Dubroca's approach. Unless the World Cup and French authorities and the refereeing controller can lay a smokescreen, then Dubroca's future as French coach must be in doubt.

The win gave British rugby a certain finalist for Twickenham in a fortnight and set up the most tumultuous occasion imaginable on Saturday, when Scotland and England meet to settle history's account.

Yesterday, the tension was almost a physical pain. England surged into a 10-3 lead in the early stages, helped by a conjuror's break from Guscott leading to a try by Underwood. But for long, long periods of the second and third quarters, England were battered by wave after blue wave.

France peeled off the back of the scrums and thundered away at short penalties, right at the heart of England. The French team is not vintage but has pace and emotion and brutality. England leant heavily on the lineout effort of Dooley and Ackford, the implacable beavering of Moore. But for a long time they were under severe pressure, and only will and guts kept them above water. The tackling of the three midfield backs, and especially of the magnificently fiery Skinner shut France out.

England are a team of above average ability, even though they lack the fiercest pace and ambition close to the scrum to conjure the tries they should from good positions. However, they are packed with courage and at this stage of the competition that virtue is so sorely needed.

Perhaps the seminal moment of the match came when France put down a five-metre scrum in the final quarter and Cecillon, the French No 8, jabbed his finger at all the

Englishmen around to warn them what he was going to do. He picked up the ball after France won the scrum and drove for the line. Skinner drove his shoulder into Cecillon's midriff, lifted him clean off his feet and dumped him back three yards.

All of this means that Blanco was denied his glorious farewell scene. Unless he changes his mind dramatically he will not be seen in Test rugby again, and one of sport's most charismatic and brilliant figures will be gone. Sadly, yesterday he should have departed after three minutes, when he had taken a late charge by Heslop. He and Champ promptly and cynically laid Heslop out.

To send off the most famous man in France on an occasion of this magnitude was beyond Mr Bishop, and I had some sympathy for him. But if Keenan, the Western Samoan, deserved to be sent off last Sunday, then Blanco deserved to go as well.

Blanco also ended the match with a cynical swallow-dive to try to win a penalty; he did not go out in style. When he came off the field, he ran straight over to embrace his tearful young son. That gesture was far more Blanco-like.

Perhaps England's best five minutes of the whole World Cup came immediately after France had levelled the match at 10-10 early in the second half with a try by Lafond in the left-hand corner. There seemed every chance that France would cut loose. They never did.

England lifted the siege. Dooley won some priceless lineouts and Hill at last took control behind the scrum. Webb kicked England into the lead with a somewhat controversial penalty five minutes from the end of normal time, and it was all beautifully sewn up in injury time when Hill chipped inch perfect to the French left-hand corner. Heslop, one of the best raiders around, caught Lafond in possession and England drove furiously over the French line. Carling, a commanding figure all day, robbed Lafond and grounded the ball.

The players celebrated joyously and, long after the teams had departed, large groups of English supporters stayed on to trumpet the victory in song all around the Parc des Princes. They had a victory of their own, too, because they had clearly outsung and outshouted the home fans during the game in support of a wonderful team performance.

Stephen Jones

FRANCE 10

S Blanco (capt); J-B Lafond, P Sella, F Mesnel, P Saint-Andre; T Lacroix, F Galthie; G Lascube, P Marocco, P Ondarts, J-M Cadieu, O Roumat, E Champ, M Cecillon, L Cabannes.

ENGLAND 19

J Webb; N Heslop, W Carling (capt), J Guscott, R Underwood, R Andrew, R Hill; J Leonard, B Moore, J Probyn, P Ackford, W Dooley, M Skinner, M Teague, P Winterbottom.

Scorers: Webb (P 5min) 0-3; Webb (P 8min) 0-6; Lacroix (P 15min) 3-6; Underwood (T 19min) 3-10; Lacroix (P 21min) 6-10; Lafond (T 51min) 10-10; Webb (P 75min) 10-13; Carling (T) & Webb (C 82min) 10-19.
Weather: sunny. Ground: excellent.
Referee: D Bishop (New Zealand).

SCOTLAND 28

G Hastings; A Stanger, S Hastings, G Shiel, I Tukalo; C Chalmers, G Armstrong; D Sole (capt), J Allan, P Burnell, C Gray, G Weir, J Jeffrey, F Calder, D White.

WESTERN SAMOA 6

A Aiolupo; B Lima, T Vaega, F Bunce, T Tagaloa; S Bachop, M Vaea; P Fatialofa (capt), S Toomalatai, V Alaalatoa, M Birtwistle, E Ioane, S Vaifale, A Perelini, P Lam.

Scorers: Vaea (P 6min) 0-3; G Hastings (P 15min) 3-3; Stanger (T 30min) 7-3; Jeffrey (T) and G Hastings (C 40min) 13-3; G Hastings (P 56min) 16-3; Bachop (DG 57min) 16-6; G Hastings (P 63min) 19-6; Jeffrey (T) and G Hastings (C 75min) 25-6; G Hastings (P 79min) 28-6.
Weather: fair. Ground: firm.
Referee: D Bevan (Wales).

THERE was no disguising the delight of the Scottish crowd as the Mexican waves swept round the stadium at half-time. And there was no disguising their warmth, either, when Western Samoa ran a lap of honour at the end.

But, equally, there could be no disguising the fact that this game was no great spectacle. Nor did it have the sense of occasion or the necessity of being there that is the stuff of international rugby today.

Still, the Samoans went down the tunnel with honour and fond memories of the triumphs of their pool games behind them. There was precious little else on offer this time, though, for Scotland shut them down remorselessly and, even when they tried their alternative game of running Fijian-style, there was no more directness from them.

Scotland went away with thoughts of the week ahead, in which they will relax as best they can and live with the prospect of the biggest game in their history only a few days away. England will come to Murrayfield next Saturday, and again the blood will be chilled by the intensity of it all. A faint heart might have survived yesterday, but next Saturday will be a day for players of steel.

Ultimately, you would have to call this match a disappointment, albeit with compensations, for the simple reason that our standards have been hoisted. Certainly, the Samoans did everything that was expected of them and we marvelled and winced at the jarring tackles of Bunce and Vaega that stopped Jeffrey and Chalmers dead. But they lacked invention and they lacked Scotland's crucial ability to tug and grind and to heave it all upfield for the short-range strikes that made such a difference at the end.

If Scotland had a plan, they certainly did not play to it. There were too many unknown factors unfolding before them, not least the wind that tortured every ball above head-height before half-time, and there had to be credit for the way they adapted to the maul.

Perhaps the crowd did bay in the last minute, when Gavin Hastings kicked an easy penalty with the game already won, but there had already been enough subtle adjustment and invention. To risk injury by battering a player over would have been rash indeed.

Afterwards, David Sole, the Scottish captain, spoke of his disappointment at aspects of the game. Of the third quarter, when the Samoans flickered life into an unconvincing comeback, he said: "I wasn't too happy. We slackened off and let them run at us."

Yet the biggest surprise of

all must have been the fact that, from the start, Scotland seemed so willing to play the game on Samoan terms. When they formed tight huddles and drove, Gray at the heart of the movement and Jeffrey fringing relentlessly, they stripped the Samoans of yards and stamina, but they were persistently guilty of spreading play needlessly and handing out invitations for their opponents to pin them down.

Gavin Hastings, and occasionally Armstrong, measured up physically, but the rest of the backs were never going to be rewarded.

Scotland came into the game with tension drawn across their faces, and they were probably surprised to find they were so far ahead at the end.

Remarkably, they had all but sewn up the game by half-time. In the first fraught minutes they gave away three points through indiscipline, when Gray questioned a decision, and they could easily have lost three more, or even their most important player, when Armstrong started throwing punches at Bunce.

As it turned out, though, they turned their backs to the wind at half-time 13-3 ahead. It was no margin to sit back on, but neither was there any suggestion that the Samoans would ever cause real difficulties, and the mêlée of their ineffectual third quarter merely confirmed suspicions.

Scotland had also scored two tries. In the 30th minute, Stanger fell on a loose ball after Chalmers had chipped ahead, and Lam, the Samoan No 8, barged his own full-back to the ground. Then, at the end of the half, Jeffrey surged round a ruck that he and Allan had set up from Armstrong's free kick.

It was fitting, on a day when Scotland were always left in command, that Jeffrey should score the try. Even more so, too, late in the game when he scored the third, his 11th for his country, for he was the most influential player throughout. When Scotland drove, he was always to the fore, and when they spread it he saved his backs embarrassment by appearing at their sides on a succession of crucial occasions.

Only in the lineouts was his presence less than convincing. But it was hardly surprising on a day when the referee, Derek Bevan of Wales, had apparently decided to ignore every lineout law ever written.

So Scotland go forward to their semi-final and possibly the most stupendous afternoon that Murrayfield will have ever seen.

Grab tickets if you can, for by Friday they will be gold dust.

There will be no rich pastures of space and opportunity at Murrayfield next Saturday, just craft and graft and possibly even grace, and the almost certain prospect of a game that will drain not only your emotions but also your dictionary of superlatives.

1991 WORLD CUP: ENGLAND RECORD NARROW VICTORY OVER SCOTS IN SEMI-FINAL

ROB JOY!

Boot-iful Andrew kicks England into World final

Andrew is glory boy

DROP OF THE HARD STUFF!

☐ WHAT A BELTER: The hero of all England — kicker Rob Andrew — sank the Scots with his deadly accuracy

Scotland 6
England 9

Victory salute: England's Mike Teague celebrates the win over Scotland. Photograph: Dave Rodgers

Defeat in last minutes breaks Scotland's heart

by James Dalrymple

UNDER lowering skies, England beat Scotland 9-6 to reach the rugby World Cup final in a tense match between the old enemies at Murrayfield yesterday.

Edinburgh was dressed in all her finery for what was in effect the northern hemisphere final of the World Cup. The flags of every nation flew over Princes Street, the city's main thoroughfare, as a dropkick by Rob Andrew gave England victory before a passionate crowd of 54,000.

In the end it was all about power and discipline against raw spirit. With just seven minutes to go, England broke

Scotland's heart. A silence settled over the huge sea of tartan, the Flower of Scotland wilted and was heard no more. And, from the 5,000 or so English fans who had entered the lion's den of Edinburgh, there suddenly was heard the sound of their adopted anthem, Swing Low Sweet Chariot.

It was a game that proved sportsmanship was not dead. A gruelling tactical affair with little open play, it was not marred by a single foul. The devastated Scots fans politely applauded the victors. The

Scottish team got a 10-minute ovation as they ran round the ground, broken and exhausted, and applauded the fans who had supported them so well.

The game had turned Edinburgh into the sporting capital of the world. Fans in their thousands arrived during the 48 hours before kick-off. Apart from the English, the bulk of the 54,000 enthusiasts from a dozen countries made it clear they were rooting for Scotland.

Early in the match, as the Scots raced into a six-point lead, the battle hymns from a
Continued on page 3

JEREMY Guscott, fresh from a gruelling 9-6 semi-final triumph over Scotland, last night repeated the "simply the best" promise he made at the start of the World Cup.

England's centre, talking exclusively to the Sunday Mirror, said before the tournament started that England would conquer the world. In the tunnel at a silenced Murrayfield yesterday, he grinned: "Yes, we're going to win the World Cup – that's a promise.

"With the Twickenham fans behind us, we are supremely confident."

New Zealand and Australia will battle it out in Dublin today for that privilege.

But on yesterday's gritty performance, a grimly determined England – who lost to the All Blacks in the opening match of the competition – will take some beating next Saturday.

Hero Rob Andrew, who kicked the dramatic winning drop goal – a world-record equalling 13th

in Tests – said: "It was a great feeling – what an encounter. Now give us Australia or New Zealand – we couldn't care less."

Captain Will Carling paid tribute to the "tremendous" Scots, but added: "They've got a superb record here – they haven't lost for 13 home games, it's a mark of how good we are.

After epic struggles against France and Scotland, questions will be asked about the stamina of England's veteran pack, often tagged "Dad's Army".

Number eight Mike Teague simply grinned: "We're not bad for a team of old men," and flanker Peter Winterbottom added: "We might not be able to run, but experience saw us through!"

Scottish coach Ian McGeechan poured cold water on English optimism, growling: "They'll have to do more than just win the ball to become world champions."

England battle to World final

A COLOSSAL effort by a superlative pack blasted England into the final of the World Cup. In an agonisingly tense game England took the lead for the first time when Andrew dropped a dramatic goal with seven minutes of normal time remaining. By then, and throughout the second half, England were in such storming control of the forward battle that there were only desperate Scottish counter-attacks to contend with in the closing minutes — and every one of those bursts was tackled to a halt.

England's maligned back row were outstanding almost beyond words. Teague, the quiet man from Gloucester, dominated the match close to the scrum and his two mates, Winterbottom and Skinner, fulfilled every dot and comma of England's pre-match plan to drive Scotland and the Scottish back row clean out of the match. We barely saw the Scotland jerseys numbered six, seven and eight all afternoon.

The English back row had the perfect platform of a fierce England scrum drive and, yet again, a spectacular line-out effort by Dooley and Ackford. The only thing certain about the final on Saturday is that England, win or lose, will be utterly exhausted when the tournament ends.

Afterwards, there were scenes of high emotion as the crowd, thank goodness, actually obeyed loudspeaker appeals not to invade the pitch. It meant that the players could hug away the ill-feeling which has grown between these two teams over the past five years. It also meant that the police could allow the Scottish team to return to the pitch for a tumultuous lap of honour to mark their exit from a tournament in which they found themselves so beautifully against Western Samoa last week, and from which, ultimately, they were muscled out — for all their wondrous effort and innovation.

It was a shame for television viewers that ITV cut away from the scenes for those uninformative interviews so beloved of television coverage which can so deflate the sense of occasion.

However, there must certainly be reservations among the sincere congratulations due to everyone in the England camp. Afterwards, there was much talk and criticism and sermonising that England were doing the game a disservice (admittedly, most of the people complaining were of nationalities which will not be represented in the World Cup final).

Still, England are now almost completely out of the habit of slipping the leash and striking hard for tries when the occasion demands it. Throughout the second half and even in the first half, they set up some beautiful attacking positions. They were not to know that their dominance in the forwards would last right until the final whistle and, with the score always so deadly close, they should have been more ambitious.

Fair enough, they scored all their points by pressurising Scotland into mistakes close to the Scottish line, but it could well have been, in a match after which there were no second chances, that they could still have come up short.

However, at Twickenham, in the World Cup final against Australia or New Zealand, they must bring off more strike moves because they will simply not be able to bludgeon and thunder the opposition out of the game.

Churning back row moves and attempts at pushover tries may not be enough. It is not so much a duty to entertain — this match was dripping with drama and tension as England played into the teeth of the loudest roaring support which can ever have been heard on a rugby ground. It is a duty to themselves to bring the best from their rich talents behind the scrum.

Scotland will be devastated, but are too realistic to ignore the fact that their scrummage and line-out work was overwhelmed on the day. It is really something for a player as brilliantly bustling as Armstrong to be kept out of the game. Armstrong gave a world-class performance against the Samoans last week, but not even he could turn the white tide breaking on his beach.

Indeed, towards the end, the Scottish effort became ragged and only Gavin Hastings' footballing excellence, power and unbreakable spirit were a danger to England. Hastings has rediscovered his form so well in this tournament that, once again, he is playing like the best full back in the game.

He did astonish friend and foe alike by missing from point-blank range in front of the posts with a penalty which would have taken Scotland back in front shortly after Webb's second goal had levelled the score. A successful pot by Hastings would have taught England that dominance without points means nothing.

Scotland tried valiantly to break up the action and to hurry England out of their steady pace and measured tread. They split their forwards at the drop-out, they threw long over short line-outs and they tried desperately to set the indomitable Sole, and the rest, running at the heart of England. But, while you can play cricket off the back foot, you simply cannot do the same in rugby.

The position for Andrew's drop goal was set up by the most likely England move of the match after a third quarter which they dominated, but in which they were showing disturbing signs of failing to cash in. They had originally set up a base camp inside the Scotland 22 when a raking kick from Guscott had made 60 yards.

Yet, although England put down a succession of five metre scrums with space available for them to attack on either side, they persisted in close-range attacks initiated by the back row. In addition, Webb, the full back — by now a rather haunted figure — had missed his third and fourth kicks at goal and, although he pulled England level after 57 minutes after Scotland had collapsed a scrum, there was the definite suspicion at the time that England could and should have gone for the try. Still, they played the percentages and they will say that they were right.

Then came that move, and Andrew's drop. It was initiated with a half-break by Andrew himself, who was cool and almost infallible as the storm of the match burst around him. He found Moore outside him and Moore sent Underwood away past two and then three defenders. It was an electric run by Underwood to celebrate his 50th cap, and Moore came storming up inside for the return pass. However, Calder managed to knock the ball away two yards from the line.

England put down more scrums and Andrew calmly fired over the drop goal. After that, there was no sign of the expected Scottish storming finale because England's pack tightened their grip until Scotland groaned.

Earlier, Scotland's attempts to impose their own game were partially successful. Hastings kicked them 6-0 into the lead with penalties against Winterbottom for offside and against Probyn for tackling Sole without the ball after a line-out. Webb pulled back three points after Scotland collapsed in the face of another English scrum drive, but there were definite signs of England control as half-time approached, and all those indicators turned into resounding actuality.

So England thunder on and Scotland depart for the third place play-off in Cardiff on Wednesday. Two seasons ago, England suffered a nightmare when Scotland crushed their Grand Slam aspirations at Murrayfield. If Scotland had prevailed again yesterday, then, in later life, England's current squad would have sat by their firesides still fretting and unfulfilled.

Yesterday, they expunged something from the memory. On Saturday, they have to wind themselves up yet again. They will have to play even better and, certainly, they will have to play wider. But at this stage of the World Cup the result, rightly, is everything and England's forwards drove magnificently for that result.

1991 WORLD CUP: AUSTRALIA BEAT ENGLAND AT TWICKENHAM IN FINAL

ENGLAND 6

WE WERE

AUSTRALIA 12

SUCKERED

POMMIE GUNS!

☐ FARR OUT: Nick Farr-Jones lifts the Trophy

England heroes go down firing

THE Rugby World Cup belongs to the Wizards of Oz . . . and England are left wondering about what might have been after losing 12-6 at windy Twickenham.

The English chariot that had swung so brilliantly through Paris and Edinburgh couldn't quite get into top gear on home soil.

But England's guns went down firing in a brave, if frustrating, battle.

So it's Nick Farr-Jones and his Aussie heroes who have the whole of the rugby world in their hands today.

There were no complaints from the England camp. Skipper Will Carling, close to tears as the fans hailed his side's effort at the finish, said:

CALIBRE

"It's been a great six weeks, a lot of hard work and it's sad it's ended this way.

"I'm proud of the way we played. The ball eluded us at vital times. At the end of the day it just wasn't going to be ours. The lads are very despondent. They'll never get another chance like this, but we'll try to lift each other and it mightn't look so bad in the morning."

England coach Roger Uttley said: "It was a great game of rugby and a final of that calibre is a credit to both teams. But we can't take anything away from Australia and there's no doubt they are worthy champions."

And England manager Geoff Cook also praised the Australians saying: "They

BRIAN MADLEY REPORTING

took their one chance and we didn't take any of ours.

"I thought we had the better of the game but couldn't get the last man free when we were on the attack."

The Wallabies walloped England 40-15 in Sydney in June but there was never going to be a repeat of that.

England changed tactics and ran the ball as often as possible. As Michael Lynagh, who scored eight of Australia's points to take his total for the tournament to 66, said: "It's was good that we had plenty of tackling practice against New Zealand last Sunday – we certainly needed it in this game."

Wade Dooley, one of the stars in the England pack, said: "I was pleased with what we did up front but the Australians defended like demons. At the end of the day the better team won."

David Campese, who had been the star of the World Cup on the run up to the final, had only one try-scoring chance but said: "I was a bit unlucky the ball didn't quite bounce right for me. But we stole one so who cares?"

☐ TALL ORDER . . . Mick Skinner stretches a point against the Wallabies' John Eales – but it's not enough to save England

Wallabies sta___
England at th___

AT THE temple of tradition, the columns of conservatism finally came crashing down as the World Cup reached a heroic new age climax. England's self-control of the past month finally yielded and they reached out for the populist tactics that could take rugby into new dimensions, a handling, passing game based on the habitual diet of possession from one of the best packs of forwards the game has ever seen.

It was not enough. Australia produced another outstanding defensive display, just as they had against the All Blacks in the semi-final, to deny England's increasingly desperate attacks from all over the field. At the heart of their defence was Tim Horan, a 21-year-old Queenslander who made a mockery of his tender age to emerge as the lionheart of the Wallabies' three-quarters.

England's new approach — they did not try a single back-row move in the first half — certainly did not lack imagination. From scrums, Carling sometimes stood in for the full-back and Halliday constantly tried to run off his wing to penetrate in mid-field. But Australia's drift defence coped with everything England's drawing board had formulated. More often than not, Horan was the player who made the vital tackle just when the advantage line seemed threatened.

It must be said that England's Brave New World did not threaten Australia's lines quite as much as the tactical think tank had hoped. First, a side used to playing to restricted patterns cannot suddenly burst forth on to the most pressurised playing field of them all and hope to achieve 100 per cent efficiency. In the first half, three hard, long passes came Underwood's way. Three times England's most capped player, their record try scorer, failed to cling on to the ball.

Second, there were moments of hesitation in mid-field, when the priority was either the quick delivery or the forthright charge straight upfield. Even the gifted Guscott stopped in his tracks once or twice, unsure of what to do next.

The result was that the game never reached the same level of pace as the All Black semi-final. The Australian back-row was never stretched quite enough to allow England's backs to enjoy a vital extra half yard of freedom after the ruck.

And even when England did manage to breach Australia's defences, there were still plenty of defenders around to halt them. In the frenzied last quarter, Eales, the apprentice from the second-row, put in a marvellous tackle in loose play to stop Andrew and end England's best movement.

When not defending, and that meant only rare moments in the first half, Australia still looked more instinctive with their attacking options. The most gifted natural footballer in their side, Campese, so nearly took advantage of his single run of the game to score the first try. Coker and Farr-Jones created space for the world record try scorer and only the bounce of the ball, after his chip ahead, prevented Campese from claiming his 47th.

His side did not have to wait much longer for their rare creativity to be rewarded, although it came after Dooley had prosaically held down Eales at a line-out and Lynagh kicked a penalty.

Five minutes later the Australian pack, bettered throughout in all aspects of play, bar the scrummage, where parity was the order of the day, combined to generate the only try of the game. Ofahengaue, conspicuous with one or two charging runs in the loose, made a vital contribution by claiming a line-out throw, two handed, a couple of yards from the English line. Supporting players drove in, spinning in-field and over the line and Daly was eventually awarded the try.

Just as England had tried to throw themselves into total rugby, it was fitting that the World Cup final should swing on the efforts of a Wallaby front-row forward, so often regarded as the supporting cast for magisterial backs.

England failed to come back into the match before half-time, Webb missing with two penalty attempts and compounding the problems of his side, who were losing the slight advantage of a fierce diagonal wind in the second period. Not that England's forwards noticed the difference. They merely tightened their stranglehold on the game. The old faithfuls,

Reaching for the skies: Captain Carling atte___

Ackford and Dooley, palmed just about everything to Hill at the line-out, while the back-row not only fished out most of the ruck ball when England were in possession, but even managed to steal a couple of balls from the Australians.

There was also a change of tactics. Teague, Hill and Skinner began to try and tie in their opposite numbers from scrums, and Winterbottom stood ever wider from second phase. And yet, it still all looked a little clumsy, one ___ Winterbottom's long pa___ floating into thin air ___ allowing Australia an ever ___ chance to counter-attack.

Their relief was short-l___ Back came England and ___ time they gained their re___ Australia were penalised ___ holding down at a line-ou___ Webb was spared abject m___ by slotting over his first pe___ in three attempts.

Only six points adrift ___ and with a quarter of an ___

d firm to stop final frontier

stop Horan, Australia's defensive lionheart, from finding touch. / Photograph by Shaun Botterill

England were poised for a ...sive comeback. But ...ralian resilience simply ... accordingly, to the extent ... they even managed to ...pe from their own half to ...ten the England line. ...agh, generally starved of ...session, yet still magnificent ...his reading of the game, ...ed delicately downwind ...ards Campo's corner, but ...bb just won the race.

...ime, however, was being ...n up in England's territory and a terrible shudder went around the ground when Australia were given a penalty after an English forward went over the top at a ruck, an echo of the infringement which haunted the early matches of this World Cup but which ultimately failed to wreck it.

Lynagh, though, ruined England's last chance with his third successful kick out of four, and despite Webb's penalty three minutes later, Australia had enough of a cushion to survive the remaining onslaught on their line.

Rugby union can look forward to its future with huge confidence. The World Cup threatened huge pressures, violence and greedy commercialism. But any game that can reach a climax such as this clash between two hemispheres and two philosophies has nothing to fear from peripheral problems. The essence of rugby has emerged scrubbed and spotless.

England: J Webb (Bath); S Halliday (Harlequins), J Guscott (Bath), W Carling (Harlequins, capt), R Underwood (Leicester); R Andrew (Wasps), R Hill (Bath); J Leonard (Harlequins), B Moore (Harlequins), J Probyn (Askeans), P Ackford (Harlequins), W Dooley (Preston Grasshoppers), M Skinner (Harlequins), P Winterbottom (Harlequins), M Teague (Gloucester).

Australia: M Roebuck (New South Wales); D Campese (New South Wales), J Little (Queensland), T Horan (Queensland), R Egerton (New South Wales); M Lynagh (Queensland), N Farr-Jones (New South Wales, capt); A Daly (New South Wales), P Kearns (New South Wales), E McKenzie (New South Wales), R McCall (Queensland), J Eales (Queensland), W Ofahengaue (New South Wales), S Poidevin (New South Wales), T Coker (Queensland).

Referee: D Bevan (Wales)

NICE TRY, WILL!

England go down fighting

■ **FARR OUT FINALE:** Aussie skipper Nick Farr-Jones lifts the World Cup

■ **PASS MASTER:** Captain courageous Will Carling leads by example to set another England attack in motion in the Twickenham final

Picture: TONY WARD

But brave England give their all

1995 WORLD CUP: ENGLAND BEAT AUSTRALIA IN QUARTER-FINAL

WILL DONE LADS

TRY-MENDOUS . . . Tony Underwood leaves Damian Smith for dead to skate in for England's try

Andrew keeps dream alive

England	25
Australia	22

FROM DAVID HANDS
RUGBY CORRESPONDENT
IN CAPE TOWN

WAS there ever a game that England sought to win so much, and won? Having done so, they must climb the same mountain all over again when they play New Zealand next Sunday, on the same Newlands ground here, in the semi-final of rugby union's World Cup.

For any English sportsman, on the southern tip of Africa or anywhere else, there have been few more heart-stopping moments than yesterday, when the 1991 finalists locked horns for the first time since that dull November day at Twickenham when Australia won the Webb Ellis trophy.

The measure of England's achievement was that not only did they dismiss the most worthy of champions from the 1995 tournament, but they also did so after losing a ten-point lead. Once, twice, they had to come from behind, and, with three minutes of added time having ticked away — and with the first extra-time game of any World Cup looming — Rob Andrew's right boot connected with one of the sweetest dropped goals he will kick throughout his career.

The whole England team raised their arms to the skies and Newlands, apparently full of their supporters judging by their rendition of the national anthem, went wild. They had suffered death by a thousand cuts during the preceding 80 minutes, but no more than the emotionally-drained team that, in the first half, had come close to realising the game it had sought to play, but had then watched as it drifted away in the face of steely opponents.

"There were two giants out there and it's not easy to weave the spells in those circumstances," Jack Rowell, the England manager, said. Until his players do, he has Andrew. The Wasps stand-off half dictated terms. He scored 20 points. He started the move which led to Tony Underwood's try. What more can one man do?

However, before praising England, Australia deserve a decent burial. How sad for the tournament that a team of their quality should leave so early.

Perhaps, as Michael Lynagh, the captain, hinted, the hunger was not the same. Certainly, the fluency was not,

yet it would be hard to overstate the quality of the game played by John Eales, the Queensland lock, who, at one stage, threatened to squeeze England out of the game single-handed.

Midway through the second half, as Australia hinted for the only time at match-winning control, the ball seemed attached to Eales as though by a string. His athleticism and the forthright play of McCall at the front of the lineout gave Australia a vision of the semi-final that, ultimately, proved so illusory. It has been a

golden era for the green-and-golds; now Lynagh, McCall and David Campese may make way for a new era; of players, and for the sport as a whole.

England, though, may bask in a warm glow. Their style may not be that to which Bob Dwyer, the Australia coach, aspires, but it served them well enough yesterday — a game based on probing use of the blind side, introducing the hard-running Carling to a perceived area of weakness just behind the Australia midfield, and the driving play of forwards, tight and loose, which forced error even from a team as sure of hand as Australia.

On a soft surface, with the smell of rain in the air and cloud hanging round Table Mountain, England lost Richards and the lead within a frenzied first four minutes. The No 8, his forehead split by a stray boot, had the flow of blood staunched and returned

only to concede the penalty with which Lynagh, shortly to become the first player to pass 900 international points, gave Australia the lead.

Immediately, England imposed themselves on the game, none more than Catt. His catching of the high ball was of the highest class, and only the strictures of a tight game-plan, which demanded field position above adventure, prevented him from running more. As it was, one delightful catch, run and kick from Campese's chip ahead

will linger in the memory.

As they had hoped, England fractured the opposing half-back link. They put Gregan under pressure, forced the errors, and Andrew kicked the goals. Two penalty goals preceded the madcap gallop of the England backs when Lynagh, of all people, dropped the ball on England's 22. Andrew gathered and sent his centres away through a broken field before Tony Underwood, on halfway, sped away from the desperate pursuit of Smith.

Had Andrew not missed a penalty goal and a dropped goal, and had Carling not rejected an overlap in favour of kicking, England's half-time advantage might have been greater. As it was, with Richards absent for running

repairs, their rhythm faltered. Lynagh stroked over a penalty goal and, within 45 seconds of the second half opening, Australia were level with a try straight out of their own game: rules football.

Lynagh spiralled a high ball into the left-hand corner and Smith, leaping above a statuesque defence, rolled over for the try.

It was the moment for Australia to regroup and for the game, apparently, to slip from England's grasp. The two stand-offs exchanged kick for kick, nerve ends twitching frantically in what Rowell later described as the "shoot-out to end all shoot-outs".

At 22-22, a dropped goal attempt from Campese flew wide — Lynagh had expected the ball on the left, where he had an overlap, but Gregan looked the other way. Instead, Catt dispatched a penalty towards the Australia 22, the ball was won, and so, thanks to Andrew, was the game.

SCORERS: **England:** Try: T Underwood. Conversion: Andrew. Penalty goals: Andrew (5). Dropped goal: Andrew. **Australia:** Try: Smith. Conversion: Lynagh. Penalty goals: Lynagh (5).
ENGLAND: M J Catt (Bath); T Underwood (Leicester), W D C Carling (Harlequins, captain), J C Guscott (Bath), R Underwood (Leicester/RAF); C R Andrew (Wasps), C D Morris (Orrell); J Leonard (Harlequins), B C Moore (Harlequins), V E Ubogu (Bath), T A K Rodber (Northampton/Army), M O Johnson (Leicester), M C Bayfield (Northampton), B B Clarke (Bath), D Richards (Leicester). Richards temporarily replaced by S O Ojomoh (Bath, 32-39min).
AUSTRALIA: M Burke (New South Wales); D I Campese (New South Wales), J S Little (Queensland), T J Horan (Queensland), D P Smith (Queensland); M P Lynagh (Queensland, captain), G M Gregan (ACT); D J Crowley (Queensland), P N Kearns (New South Wales), E J A McKenzie (New South Wales), V Ofahengaue (New South Wales), R J McCall (Queensland), J A Eales (Queensland), D J Wilson (Queensland), B T Gavin (New South Wales).
Referee: D J Bishop (New Zealand).

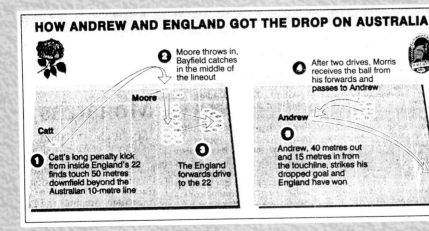

HOW ANDREW AND ENGLAND GOT THE DROP ON AUSTRALIA

❷ Moore throws in, Bayfield catches in the middle of the lineout

❹ After two drives, Morris receives the ball from his forwards and passes to Andrew

Moore

Andrew

Catt

❶ Catt's long penalty kick from inside England's 22 finds touch 50 metres downfield beyond the Australian 10-metre line

❸ The England forwards drive to the 22

❺ Andrew, 40 metres out and 15 metres in from the touchline, strikes his dropped goal and England have won

BOOT

Golden shot

● LAST gasp hero Rob Andrew collects Dewi Morris's perfect lay-back pass and launches his mighty drop-goal towards the Aussie posts.

ROB ANDREW landed the greatest kick of his life here yesterday to send England into the World Cup semi-finals with a sensational injury-time drop goal.

As it soared sweetly between the posts there were two minutes of injury-time already showing on the digital clock. And though Australia battled back like wounded animals for one last desperate fling, they knew it was all over.

The holders were out — and now Will Carling's dream of winning the World Cup moves on to a crunch clash with the awesome All Blacks back here next Sunday.

When Kiwi referee David Bishop finally ended the most dramatic of the four quarter-finals, grown men from both sides sank to their knees and unashamedly wept either tears of joy or despair.

Martin Bayfield and Ben Clarke threw themselves full length on the ground, sizzling try-scorer Tony Underwood punched the air and Andrew did a little jig of delight.

Yesterday as thousands of singing fans turned Newlands into a foreign Twickenham, England gained revenge for their 12-6 final defeat of four years ago.

They even had a bonus of seeing David Campese sending a feeble drop-goal chance wide only moments earlier.

Amazing

Poor Campo looked as though he had gone a competition too far. Apart from a couple of monster touch finders he only had one run — and then a mere lock, Martin Bayfield, cut him down.

But Bayfield's real heroics were to come in those amazing final seconds after England had been hauled back from 13-3 to 22-22 through a brilliant try by wing Damian Smith.

With extra-time looming, England gained a line-out 45 yards from the Aussie line and up went the 6ft10ins Bayfield, who had generally been outjumped by John Eales.

This time the Englishman's telescopic reach dragged the ball out of the sky, the England pack drove in and rammed the Aussies back 15 crucial yards to put the posts in reach of the deadliest right foot in world rugby.

Dewi Morris's lay-back pass was perfect — and so too was Andrew's soaring drop goal to extend his own world record drop goal tally to 21.

All England had to do then was hold their nerve for a couple more frantic seconds — and they did that comfortably.

Both teams scored a fabulous try, world record points scorer Michael Lynagh had matched Andrew's five penalties and a conversion in passing 900 Test points. But once again the England hero was Prince Andrew.

England might have had the

IT'S THERE! Andrew turns away to celebrate as his brilliant kick sails through the posts to clinch a truly magnificent victory

Prince Andrew is the last action hero

COLIN PRICE
reports from Cape Town

match won by half-time had they used their stream of top quality possession more wisely instead of kicking it away too often.

But it was impossible to fault the heart of the Grand Slam winners as Australia came back like true champions.

England went off like a fire-cracker but it was the Aussies who struck the first blow when Dewi Morris was penalised for delaying the put-in at the first scrum as he tried to buy time while Dean Richards had a nasty head-wound bandaged.

Lynagh stepped up to send his simple kick through the posts.

Two minutes later Andrew

cancelled that out when Jeremy Guscott lost his footing in trying to slice his way through from Tim Rodber's line-out ball and in their eagerness to snap the possession up Australia strayed off-side.

Martin Johnson's line-out take gave Andrew a second penalty for a 6-3 lead and the first signs of worry began appearing on Aussie faces.

Pressure

Morris was forced into touch by Rod McCall as he tried to spin down the blind-side of one scrum and Andrew wasted one glorious chance to stretch the Aussie defence when he elected to take a drop at goal from and sent the ball wide with two men screaming outside him.

But the pressure finally paid off in the most thrilling style though when the break came from a wonderful counter-attack.

Lynagh worked a loop

around Jason Little but dropped the ball. Andrew snaffled it and with a flick-pass sent Guscott away. He handed on to Carling and suddenly the ball was in Tony Underwood's hands with the first real room of the match.

He needed only one look to see the outside was vulnerable and left both Smith and Matt Burke for dead with a 60-yard dash to glory.

Long before he had completed the run, full back Mike Catt had raised both hands in jubilation. And when Andrew knocked over the wide-angled conversion England were ahead at 13-3 after 22 minutes.

Andrew missed his only kick of the match three minutes later when Lynagh was penalised for not releasing and England began to realise their safety-cushion wasn't padded enough.

Two minutes into first-half injury-time Lynagh knocked

over a 35 metre penalty when Rodber got offside in tackling George Gregan.

That made it 13-6 at the break — and within 60 seconds of the re-start it was all square thanks to an astonishing catch by Smith.

The Queensland wing, preferred to teenage prodigy Joe Roff, hared after a wicked high kick from Lynagh and as Catt waited under the ball Smith leapt Aussie-rules style to snatch the ball high above his head, fall to the ground and roll over.

Lynagh converted and within the space of 90 seconds either side of half time England had seen their comfort zone of two scores swept away.

Edgy

At times like that you learn what teams are made of and the England pack produced another terrific rolling maul which forced the Aussies to collapse and Andrew kicked a routine penalty to make it 16-13.

Two minutes later the over-eager Johnson strayed off-side and Lynagh's penalty levelled the scores.

Rory Underwood missed a good breakaway chance and England paid dearly for that. Victor Ubogo piled in over the top of a ruck and Lynagh kicked the penalty — 19-16 with 22 minutes left.

Straight from the re-start Australia infringed and Andrew dropped his 38-metre penalty over from a difficult angle —19-19.

With 17 minutes left Rodber was again penalised, this time harshly, for his challenge on

Smith, and Lynagh nosed Australia in front ahead 22-19.

England's began to look decidedly edgy. Andrew was just wide with a monster penalty from the half-way line, Catt sent an equally ambitious drop goal wide — and there were only five minutes left for England to save themselves.

Then Catt boomed one into the air, Burke caught well but Moore snatched the ball from his hands and Australia in their desperation to defend the line, strayed offside.

There is no cooler customer in the world in situations like these than Andrew. All he needs is a sniff of a chance. The Aussies gave him two in those last five frantic minutes.

He knocked over the penalty from 22 metres to level the scores again — then sent an estimated 10million armchair viewers back home wild with that great drop goal.

WORLD CUP SEMI-FINALS
Saturday June 17, Durban, 2pm
FRANCE
v
S. AFRICA
Sunday June 18, Cape Town, 2pm
NEW ZEALAND
v
ENGLAND

1995 WORLD CUP: ALL BLACKS OUTPLAY ENGLAND IN SEMI-FINAL

SO LONG SWEET CHARIOT

England at end of road

Try, try, try and try again: Lomu leaves Andrew trailing, main photograph, to score his second try in Cape Town yesterday. The New Zealand wing broke England's resistance by scoring four, inset

All Blacks sweep into World Cup final with powerful display

Lomu runs England ragged

England 29
New Zealand 45

FROM DAVID HANDS
RUGBY CORRESPONDENT
IN CAPE TOWN

AND when they awoke from the nightmare, England found it was all true. Yesterday, at Newlands, where a week earlier they had sent the 1991 champions, Australia, packing from the Rugby World Cup, they conceded everything but pride to a New Zealand side that will return to the high veld of Transvaal on Saturday to contest the 1995 final with South Africa.

Never before have England conceded 45 points, but nor have they come up against the monstrous behemoth that is Jonah Lomu. The 18½-stone wing scored four of New Zealand's six tries and not one England defender was able to lay a hand on him; whatever price the newly rich rugby league scouts placed on his head before the weekend, they can double it now.

Nor should England pretend that the 16-point margin represents the true difference between the teams. They were out-thought, outrun, outmuscled and, if New Zealand had been playing the final, they would surely have focused far more intently during the last quarter when England scored their four tries. Instead, at 35-3, they relaxed to save themselves for the final effort at Ellis Park against their southern hemisphere confrères.

This was the stylistic triumph that Laurie Mains wanted. The All Blacks coach put this side together in a series of training camps over their summer (and almost left Lomu out as a disciplinary measure). Critics suggested — before yesterday — that it had not been thoroughly tested against Canada (at home), Ireland,

Japan, Wales and Scotland. But that England, one of the top four teams in the world, should be so humiliated is a complete vindication. At no stage did the Englishmen come to terms with the speed of thought of the All Blacks, with the lines of running and with the support which pours in so closely behind the man in possession. Moreover, they lacked a set-piece game through which they could exert some authority because New Zealand did not allow them one, until it suited them.

There were, for example, only nine productive lineouts in the first half and only two more in the second. Martin Bayfield was closed out of the game and, if the All Blacks had been just a little more disciplined, the score would have soared past the half-century. Instead, both Robin Brooke and Dowd were warned for foul play and England, with a second-half advantage in penalties of 10-2, were able to gather some momentum.

However, the game had gone way beyond them by then, starting from the moment New Zealand kicked off away from their forwards and to-

wards Lomu's wing, where Tony Underwood and Carling collided. Having seized the tactical and territorial initiative, the All Blacks seldom relinquished it. Within three minutes, Bachop's long pass had found Lomu and the wing's hand-off disposed of Underwood, his deceptive pace dealt with Carling and his sheer strength overwhelmed Catt.

From the restart, Guscott missed Little and the powerful centre was away, linking with Osborne until the ubiquitous Kronfeld hove into sight. If ever England needed the benison of points, it was now, but Andrew, a rock throughout this tournament, foundered with a dropped goal and a penalty and then had to watch as

Mehrtens kicked over from 46 metres and Zinzan Brooke dropped a goal from Carling's poor clearance.

When Osborne sent Lomu to the line for his second try, New Zealand were 25 points ahead in as many minutes and the contest was over. With his third attempt, Andrew kicked a penalty, but, if England hope flickered briefly, the light was extinguished when Mehrtens kicked behind the defence, Little gathered and Lomu strode over again.

A delightfully contrived back-row move created Bachop's try and all that was left for England was blind pride. Inspired by Morris and Clarke, they were able to establish field positions. A shade fortuitously, since his feet seemed in touch before he dotted down, Rory Underwood was awarded a try and twice Carling followed him over as England threw caution to the wind.

In between Carling's brace, however, Lomu became the first player to score four tries against England since Maurice Richards for Wales in 1969. Bachop began it with the interception and, though time remained for Rory Underwood to cross for a second time, the banner which heralded "Sir Rob" had long since been folded up as England's vociferous supporters started to plan their departure.

SCORERS: England: Tries: Carling (2), R Underwood (2). Conversions: Andrew (3). Penalty goal: Andrew. New Zealand: Tries: Lomu (4), Kronfeld, Bachop. Conversions: Mehrtens (3). Penalty goal: Mehrtens. Dropped goals: Z Brooke, Mehrtens.

ENGLAND: M J Catt (Bath); T Underwood (Leicester), W D C Carling (Harlequins, captain), J C Guscott (Bath), R Underwood (Leicester/RAF); C R Andrew (Wasps), C D Morris (Orrell); J Leonard (Harlequins), B C Moore (Harlequins), V E Ubogu (Bath), T A K Rodber (Northampton/Army), M O Johnson (Leicester), M C Bayfield (Northampton), B B Clarke (Bath), D Richards (Leicester).

NEW ZEALAND: G M C·sborne (North Harbour); J W Wilson (Otago), F E Bunce (North Harbour), W K Little (North Harbour), J T Lomu (Counties); A Mehrtens (Canterbury), G T M Bachop (Canterbury); C Dowd (Auckland), S B T Fitzpatrick (Auckland, captain), O M Brown (Auckland), M R Brewer (Canterbury), I D Jones (North Harbour), R M Brooke (Auckland), J Kronfeld (Otago), Z V Brooke (Auckland), Z Brooke replaced by B P Larsen (North Harbour, 65min).

Referee: S R Hilditch (Ireland)

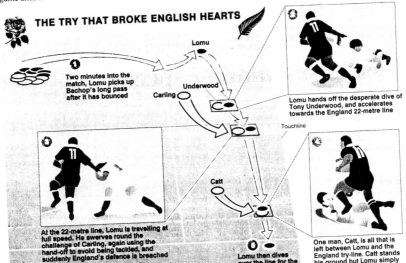

THE TRY THAT BROKE ENGLISH HEARTS

Lomu

Underwood

Carling

1 Two minutes into the match, Lomu picks up Bachop's long pass after it has bounced

Lomu hands off the desperate dive of Tony Underwood, and accelerates towards the England 22-metre line

Touchline

Catt

At the 22-metre line, Lomu is travelling at full speed. He swerves round the challenge of Carling, again using the hand-off to avoid being tackled, and suddenly England's defence is breached

Lomu then dives over the line for the first of his four tries

One man, Catt, is all that is left between Lomu and the England try-line. Catt stands his ground but Lomu simply runs through his tackle

GRAPHIC: LAURA SYLVESTER

JUNE 18 1995

MOORE MISERY — England hooker Brian Moore troops off the pitch looking devastated after taking a real battering from the magnificent All Blacks

CLAPPED OUT — Dewi Morris and Will Carling pay tribute to New Zealand at the end, and the England skipper clearly nose (right) we were outplayed

LOMU TOP OF LEAGUE

By PHIL THOMAS

ALL BLACK sensation Jonah Lomu can change codes and prove himself the most dynamic talent ever to play Rugby League.

Leeds are the latest club lining up a £1million bid. Wigan, Auckland Warriors and Sydney Bulldogs are all keen and there is also a £4m offer for him to play American Football.

Scouts from just about every club in England are in South Africa hunting new blood.

Salford player-coach Andy Gregory said: "As far as I'm concerned there is only one man any top club should go for at any price — and that's Jonah.

"Will Carling had it just about right when he called him a freak. That's exactly what he is. No one that size has that speed and that ability. He is just phenomenal."

But New Zealand manager Brian Lachore insists the All Blacks would do everything possible to prevent Lomu from changing codes.

Lachore said: "I am sure that our Prime Minister will put up the Crown Jewels to keep him in our game."

While All Blacks team manager Colin Meads growled: "You don't become a great player in one year or in one game. We can start calling him great in a couple of years."

Mains also expressed concern about their leaking defence after they conceded three tries against Ireland and Scotland and four against England.

He said: "I am worried about our defence. It would have been better if we had attacked more."

LOMURDER

He is a freak. I hope I never see him again

– WILL CARLING AFTER JONAH SINKS ENGLAND

England 29 New Zealand 45